CHINESE REGIONAL COOKING

THE CHINESE COOKERY & THINGS
P. O. Box 19300
Oakland, CA 94619-0300

CHINESE REGIONAL COOKING

Authentic Recipes from the Liang School

By Lucille Liang

Sterling Publishing Co., Inc.   New York

ACKNOWLEDGMENTS

I want to express my deepest gratitude to all my cooking class students, whose wholehearted support and enthusiasm make this book possible. I am also thankful to my student Jeanne Chretien for her careful and professional typing of the manuscript, to my family for their understanding and support, and last but not least, to the following students for their most helpful comments and encouragement: Reverend Dahl B. Seckinger, District Superintendent, The Christian and Missionary Alliance; Robert Goldstein, Registrar, City University of New York; Nina Enthoven, Advertising Copywriter, McCann-Erickson; Richard DeBritt, Vice Consul, Australian Consulate-General; Rimfa England, Corporate Attorney; Raleigh D'Adamo, Transportation Commissioner, Westchester County, as well as countless others whom I do not have space here to name individually.

Color photography by Frank Ledermann, The Upstairs Photography Studio, Bronxville, New York.

Drawings by Alex Chin.

First Paperback Printing, 1982

Copyright © 1979 by Sterling Publishing Co., Inc.
Two Park Avenue, New York, N.Y. 10016
Distributed in Australia by Oak Tree Press Co., Ltd.
P.O. Box J34, Brickfield Hill, Sydney 2000, N.S.W.
Distributed in the United Kingdom by Blandford Press
Link House, West Street, Poole, Dorset BH15 1LL, England
Distributed in Canada by Oak Tree Press Ltd.
% Canadian Manda Group, 215 Lakeshore Boulevard East
Toronto, Ontario M5A 3W9
Manufactured in the United States of America
All rights reserved
Library of Congress Catalog Card No.: 79-65067
Sterling ISBN 0-8069-0148-9 Trade
0149-7 Library
7574-1 Paper

CONTENTS

Color section follows page 96.

CONTENTS BY
FOOD CATEGORIES

I. Hors D'Oeuvres

II. Soups

III. Fish and Seafood

IV. Meat (Pork and Beef)

V. Poultry and Eggs

VI. Vegetables and Bean Curd

VII. Rice, Noodles, Dumplings, and other *Dim Sum*

VIII. Desserts

FOREWORD

Lucille Liang has been teaching authentic Chinese cooking for years, and she has lectured extensively on Chinese cooking and culture. She is a super cook and teacher.

As a student of hers, I am fortunate not only in learning her many recipes and skillful techniques but to enjoy the traditions and cultural background she tells with each recipe. After much prodding by her students, she has written her first cookbook of over 100 recipes arranged by their regions of origin. This book is more than a culinary experience; it is a total cultural education in the art of Chinese cooking and dining.

Mrs. Liang's recipes of the classical Chinese dishes are exceptional—the best I have ever tasted. Her recipes for Fried Dumplings are without equal, as are the Hot and Sour Soup, Kung Pao Chicken and Spicy Shredded Beef with Cellophane Noodles, just to mention a few. Mrs. Liang has presented the techniques of Chinese cooking in a clear, easily understandable manner so that even the novice can produce a delicious dish on first try.

For those who have never tried the stir-fry cooking method, as a practicing physician, I highly recommend it as a very nutritious way of cooking. Stir-fry cooking is the best way to retain the natural vitamins and minerals in foods. In the near future it will probably become a common technique in American kitchens.

Many of my colleagues and I have taken to cooking as a relaxing, diverting hobby. I trust that this book will lead you to a rewarding, enjoyable, gastronomic, nutritional and cultural experience as it has for her students.

PAUL J. LOMBARDI, M.D.

PREFACE

Inspired and encouraged by hundreds of my cooking school students and many hundreds of others who have tried my recipes, I have decided to compile my well-loved and tested recipes to form an authentic Chinese cookbook. But this is not simply "another Chinese cookbook." It is interesting and unique because in addition to giving authentic delicious recipes, it offers the following added features.

First of all, the recipes are written in a simple, clear, easy-to-follow style that leads to successful and rewarding results. Many of my American students and friends have tried recipes from different Chinese cookbooks and they all seemed to have confronted the same troubles: the recipes were too "wordy" or "unnecessarily complicated," and many dishes simply did not come out right. Some of these people were so discouraged by the long "preparation" section that they simply stopped cooking Chinese food. The recipes in this book are not merely simply and clearly written, they have also been tested by hundreds of my students with excellent results.

Secondly, the recipes are not arranged by the traditional method, that is, listing foods by categories: soups, chicken, meat, fish, vegetables, and so on. Instead, they are arranged by the four major schools of cooking in China: Eastern (Shanghai Style), Northern (Peking Style), Western (Szechuan and Hunan Style), and Southern (Canton Style), with a separate chapter for hors d'oeuvres and desserts. Americans are far more sophisticated now than they were in the 1960s, and many of them are sampling and enjoying more exotic dishes from Szechuan, Shanghai, and Peking in addition to the more familiar delicious Cantonese dishes. It will be easier for them to find a particular regional dish that they wish to cook, with this method of organization. Furthermore, recipes that belong to the same region are arranged by ease of preparation so that a beginner can start with an easy recipe and then move on confidently to more intricate banquet-style dishes.

Thirdly, wherever possible, a short story behind each dish or an interesting episode about the ingredients used precedes the recipe. From my experience in teaching cooking, I find that students want to know not only the basic techniques, but also the cultural and historical background behind them. By relating the backgrounds of the dishes, I feel that the American cook will be more interested and will want to try the dishes more eagerly.

Furthermore, at the end of most recipes, a special "Note" is included to make preparation easier. Through these notes the cook is advised which procedures can be done ahead of time, which dishes can be made several hours earlier or even frozen, how to make cooking easier, and what substitutions can be made to vary a dish or replace an ingredient that is unavailable. Since Chinese cooking is infinitely variable, every recipe given here can be turned into several different recipes, once you have mastered the basic techniques.

The color photos show how to arrange the dishes attractively, since presentation and color, in addition to good aroma and delicious flavor, are important elements of any good Chinese dish. Many Americans know how to cook certain Chinese dishes, but they have neglected to make them presentable. For example, Assorted Cold Platter, usually the first course in a Chinese banquet, would be merely an unattractive hodge-podge if not arranged and presented in special ways.

Sample menus given at the back of the book show how to choose dishes from different regions to form a tasty and well-balanced meal. Indeed, balance is essential in enjoying Chinese food to the full extent. One Szechuan dish in a meal is fine; two might be one too many for some people. The meats of the Northern region and the seafood of the Eastern area may be balanced with stir-fried dishes from Canton. Intricate banquet-style dishes may be blended with the simple, but equally authentic home-cooked dishes. Variety is really the essence of Chinese cooking.

In addition, the dishes presented in this book are nutritious and healthful. No MSG and a minimum of oil is used in the recipes. Overall, large amounts of vitamin- and mineral-rich vegetables are combined with relatively small quantities of meat. The recipes should not only delight beginners and advanced cooks alike, but also those calorie- and health-conscious Americans. And since the most frequently used cooking technique is quick stir-frying, precious fuel and energy are saved.

All in all, the recipes in this book take advantage of my years of experience in teaching the art of Chinese cooking. The genuine cooking methods are firmly rooted in Chinese tradition. But my aim is not merely to teach Americans how to cook authentic Chinese dishes; I hope that, by reading the book and following the recipes, you will not only enjoy flavorful, nutritious Chinese dishes, but also will get to know more about the Chinese people and their traditions. And I hope that this cookbook will bring pleasure not only to my students but also to all those whom I cannot reach with my cooking classes.

LUCILLE LIANG

INTRODUCTION:
THE FOUR MAJOR SCHOOLS
OF COOKING IN CHINA

During a recent visit to Taipei and Hong Kong, I was invited to dine in a different restaurant almost every evening. Out of hospitality and courtesy, the host and hostess often checked with me to find out which particular regional food I like best in order to know which restaurant they would bring me to. I was surprised, and in a way pleased, to find that the four major schools of cooking are still as prevalent in China as ever. A good restaurant is often known for one school of cooking, and people who want to sample authentic regional dishes clearly know where to go.

For years the only Chinese cooking Americans knew was Cantonese because Cantonese people were the first to emigrate. With the historic first visit of an American president to China in 1972 and the ensuing explosion of interest in Chinese food and cooking, Americans realized that there existed a great variety of exotic regional foods which they had never tried. Sophisticated Americans began to sample hot and spicy dishes from Szechuan and Hunan; rich, red-cooked dishes from the eastern cities of Shanghai, Soochow, and Yangchow; light and delicate banquet dishes from Hopei and Shantung provinces; as well as authentic stir-fried dishes from Canton.

In order to fully appreciate and enjoy the different styles of cooking, a brief description of the development and the special features of each of the four schools of cooking follows.

The eastern region of China, especially in the provinces Kiangsu and Chekiang, is best known for its red-cooking method—cooking with dark soy sauce by low heat. Kiangsu and Chekiang cooking centers in Shanghai, spreading out to Soochow, Hangchow, and Yangchow. Soochow cooking uses a little extra sugar for sweetness. Hangchow is famous for freshwater fish and shellfish. Yangchow, the business center in the old days, is known for its northern style of pastry (called *dim sum* by the Cantonese), and for special dishes such as Yangchow Fried Rice and Yangchow Lion's Head.

Since the eastern region is by the sea, seafood and meat dishes are equally available. Eastern cooking is further enhanced by an abundance of vegetables, including fresh bamboo shoots, which are delicate in texture and taste.

The northern style of cooking developed primarily in Hopei, Honan, and Shantung provinces. Today the center of northern cooking is Peking, which was the location of the Imperial Court for many centuries. Since the best cooking was supposed to have been done in the Imperial Palace or capital city, many banquet dishes are from the northern region. Generally, northern cooking tends to be light and mild. Wine stock is frequently used for its prestigious and delicate flavor; leek, scallions, and garlic are favored seasoning. Typical dishes are Peking Duck, Fillet of Fish with Wine Rice Sauce, Mu Shu Pork, and Hot and Sour Soup.

Furthermore, since wheat, rather than rice, is the staple of the northern area, northerners are experts in making noodle dishes and dumplings such as fried dumplings, steamed dumplings, and boiled dumplings (*shui jiao* or *suey gow*). Although garlic and scallions are very commonly used, as a whole, northern food is less spicy and less oily than that of the western region. Foods are generally cooked medium, neither well-done, as in the eastern region, nor underdone, as in the southern region. Northern cooking is actually quite hearty and wholesome.

Szechuan and Hunan provinces, the western region of China, were neither near the sea, like Shanghai city, nor near the Imperial Court, like Peking. Until recently, food from this area was not very well known. The outstanding feature of the food from this region is that it is hot and spicy. This is understandable because the weather in western China is hot and humid, and spices of all kinds grow well there. Mushrooms are abundant because of rainfall. The Szechuan peppercorn, a delicate, aromatic spice, is the region's famous product, and the chili pepper is a distinctive spice.

In this region, oil is generally used with hot spices to seal in the taste of the ingredients. Hot sauces of various kinds are served with the dishes. In addition, hot spices are mixed with scallion and garlic to increase the flavor of the food. Chengtu, the capital of Szechuan province, is often called Little Peking because of its many good restaurants. Typical Szechuan dishes are Kung Pao Chicken (Chicken with Hot Pepper), Crispy Spicy Fish, Fish-Flavored Chicken, Dry-Cooked String Beans, and Ma Po Bean Curd. An interesting point to mention here is that although spiciness is the outstanding feature of daily meals, formal dinners or banquets in Szechuan rarely include any hot or spicy courses.

A household Chinese saying states, "Good food comes from Canton." Canton, the capital of Kwangtung, is ideally suited for becoming a center of culinary excellence. Its climate favors agriculture. Plentiful feed for livestock makes high quality meat abundant. Located on the seacoast, Canton also has an ample supply of seafood. Furthermore, the Cantonese love to eat and enjoy good food. Generally speaking, they prefer to spend money on food rather than on clothes, housing, or silly vanities. Delicious, well-prepared food is first priority. Another characteristic of the Cantonese people is that they are adventurous, and hence are innovative and creative in cooking. Many exciting new dishes are developed by the gourmet cooks of Canton, and there are endless varieties of food designed for various appetites.

Stir-frying and blanching are the most popular cooking methods. In addition, southern cooking is also well known for dishes braised in dark soy sauce and roasted for hot or cold plates, such as roast pork, roast duck, and roast chicken. Well-known southern dishes include Shark's Fin Soup, Shrimp with Cashew Nuts, Steamed Fish with Fermented Black Beans, Stuffed Bean Curd, and Beef in Oyster Sauce with Snow Peas and Water Chestnuts.

In summary, Chinese cooking can be divided into four regional styles. Regional dishes can be identified not only by the cooking methods used, but also by the ingredients and condiments special to each region. The reader should be aware that he or she is luckier than the people who developed these cuisines, in that most

Chinese rarely had a chance to taste food from regions outside their own. Until recently, transportation and communication between areas ranged from poor to nonexistent. Today those adventurous Americans who love Chinese food not only can taste different regional dishes at restaurants but also can try their hands at cooking these dishes at home, since authentic Chinese ingredients are available now in supermarkets and in an ever-growing number of Chinese grocery stores all over the country.

On the other hand, it should also be pointed out that there are many national dishes common throughout China. They are equally enjoyed and appreciated by the Chinese at banquet dinners and at daily family meals.

The following chapters cover a wealth of authentic and delicious regional dishes that exemplify the four major schools of cooking in China. I am sure that American cooks, having been informed about the interesting background of these four regions, will be eager to try their hands at cooking these exotic and tasty dishes.

BEFORE YOU START

Here is some important information that you will need to know before you start to cook.

First of all, authentic ingredients like Chinese rice wine (Shao Shing Wine) instead of dry sherry, and tapioca starch instead of cornstarch, are used in all the recipes. This is so because Chinese ingredients are extremely important in Chinese cooking. It is these ingredients, together with all the other authentic ingredients used in this book, that make the dishes taste authentically Chinese. Cooking with wine is a time-honored Chinese tradition. Wine is used to enhance the flavor of a dish as well as to neutralize the odor of food. In China the wine used for cooking comes from Shao Shing and is named for that city.

When most of the other Chinese cookbooks were published, authentic Chinese ingredients were hard to come by and therefore substitutes were often mentioned. Due to the explosion of interest in Chinese cooking in the early 1970s, many more Chinese food products are available in supermarkets and in an ever-growing number of Chinese specialty stores throughout the country. More interesting and authentic dishes can now be made.

As you try the recipes, you will find that the genuine ingredients are much better in many ways. For instance, tapioca starch is much lighter than cornstarch. Tapioca starch can be used to tenderize meat and, when used as a thickening agent, will add a glaze to food.

If you do not have any Chinese grocery stores near you, mail orders are accepted at Liang's Oriental Gifts and Grocery Inc., 8 Pleasantville Road, Pleasantville, N.Y. 10570. Telephone (914) 769-6611.

Second, when you double or triple the recipes, generally you will need to double or triple every ingredient accordingly. There is an exception to this rule though; you do not need to double the oil exactly. For instance, if normally 2 tablespoons of oil is called for, when you double the recipe you do not need to use 4 tablespoons of oil; instead, 3 tablespoons is sufficient for the purpose. For those people who are on a low-sodium diet, the amount of salt need not be doubled strictly. Quantities of seasonings have been prescribed to suit general tastes, but you may decide you like more or less salt, sugar, and so forth.

Finally, everything in this book will work successfully if you follow the directions and procedures carefully. But do read the recipes several times before you attempt the dishes. Furthermore, do not try a recipe for the first time at a dinner party. Always cook each recipe for the family before trying it for company. Finally, a small but important point often overlooked by many is that "Tbs" is "tablespoon" and "tsp" is "teaspoon."

Each recipe alone will serve about four people when served with one or more other dishes, as is usually the case.

PART I

Dishes Typical of Eastern China (Shanghai Style)

Empress Chicken 貴妃鷄翅

Since "Empress" shows imperial qualification, this dish definitely ranks as a high-quality main dish. Chicken wings (without tips), dried mushrooms, and bamboo shoots are all considered best ingredients, and they make a lovely presentation glistening under the tasty glazed sauce.

INGREDIENTS:

8 *large chicken wings (about 2 lb or 1 kg)*
3 *Tbs dark soy sauce*
2 *Tbs Chinese rice wine*
½ *tsp salt* } *to marinate chicken wings*
2 *tsp sugar*
2 *cloves star anise*
10 *dried Chinese mushrooms*
½ *cup winter bamboo shoots*
1 *scallion*
one 1-inch (2½-cm) piece ginger root
1 *Tbs peanut or vegetable oil*
½ *cup chicken broth*
1 *Tbs tapioca starch dissolved in 2 Tbs cold water*

PROCEDURES:

1. Cut each chicken wing at the joint and discard wing tips. Wash and dry well. Marinate with soy sauce, wine, salt, sugar, and star anise for about 30 minutes. Reserve the marinade for later use.

2. Soak the mushrooms in hot water to soften for 20 minutes; cut off and discard the stems, then cut each top in half. Roll-cut the bamboo shoots into 1-inch (2½-cm) pieces. Cut the scallion into 2-inch-long (5-cm) sections; peel and then crush the ginger root with flat side of cleaver.

TO COOK:

3. Heat the oil in a heavy saucepan or Dutch oven over medium heat. Add the ginger and then the wings. Stir-fry the chicken wings for about 30 seconds to seal. Then add the reserved marinade and stir to coat the wings. Add the scallion, bamboo shoots, and mushrooms and stir for 2 more minutes. Then add chicken broth, bring to a boil, cover and simmer over medium heat for about 30 minutes, stirring occasionally.

4. Arrange the chicken wings in the center of a serving platter and place the mushrooms and bamboo shoots at the left and right of the wings, respectively. Thicken the sauce in the saucepan with 1 Tbs tapioca starch dissolved in 2 Tbs cold water. Pour the glazed sauce over the chicken, mushrooms, and bamboo shoots. Serve hot.

NOTE: This dish can be cooked ahead of time and left in saucepan. Just before serving, warm the chicken and vegetables thoroughly on the stove and then follow step 4 to finish the dish. A wok can be used instead of the saucepan.

Agar-Agar Salad with Ham 拌菜拌大腿

One of the main dishes at a meal, a Chinese salad is more than a mixture of raw vegetables. Meat and eggs, which need cooking, are often included among the ingredients. This Agar-Agar Salad with Ham is lovely to look at with its four contrasting colors: the red ham, the light green Chinese cabbage, the white agar-agar, and the yellow egg strips. This cold plate is also very nutritious. One of the ingredients, agar-agar, is a processed and dried seaweed, and is therefore high in iodine. In the days before the introduction of gelatin, agar-agar was used as a thickening agent to make cold jellied dishes. When soaked in boiling-hot water, it melts into a gelatinous substance. But after being soaked in cold water, it becomes bouncy and crunchy, making it an excellent ingredient to mix with meat, chicken, and vegetables.

INGREDIENTS:

1 egg
1 tsp Chinese rice wine
¼ lb (125 g) Smithfield ham
½ oz (15 g) agar-agar strips
½ lb (250 g) Chinese cabbage
½ Tbs peanut or vegetable oil
1 Tbs light soy sauce ⎫
½ tsp salt |
2 tsp sugar ⎬ *combined seasoning sauce*
1 Tbs white rice vinegar |
1 Tbs sesame oil ⎭

PROCEDURES:

1. Beat the egg thoroughly with the wine. Set aside for 30 minutes.

2. Remove skin and fat from the Smithfield ham. Boil the ham for about 10 minutes. Cool, then shred into 2-inch (5-cm) strips.

3. Cut the agar-agar with scissors into 2-inch (5-cm) lengths. Soak in cold water to cover for about 10 minutes. Drain and squeeze out the water. Wash and shred the Chinese cabbage, then mix with agar-agar.

TO COOK:

4. Heat the wok very hot. Turn heat down to low and allow the wok to cool for 2 minutes. Pour in ½ Tbs oil and swirl around the wok. Pour in half of the beaten egg with wine, swirl around the wok until a thin round egg sheet forms. Flip the sheet over and fry about 30 seconds more. Transfer to a plate and cool. Repeat with other half of the egg mixture. Shred the egg sheet into 2-inch (5-cm) strips.

5. Combine the sauce ingredients. Just before serving, pour the sauce over the agar-agar and cabbage mixture and mix well in a bowl. Transfer to a serving plate and top with the shredded ham and then the shredded egg strips. Serve cold.

NOTE: The salad can be made ahead of time and refrigerated, but add the sauce just before serving. Canned abalone and cooked chicken may be shredded and added to the salad.

Fish Balls and Bean Threads Soup　魚丸粉絲湯

A light and delicate soup, this dish is easy to make and yet delicious and nutritious. Bean threads, or cellophane noodles, are made from powdered mung beans and are therefore rich in vitamins. Although customarily called "noodles" by Americans, these threads are really a vegetable product and are often used in soups, and in stir-fried and simmered dishes.

INGREDIENTS:

2 oz (60 g) bean threads (cellophane noodles)
1 8-oz (250 g) package frozen fish balls
4 cups chicken broth
1 Tbs fish sauce
salt and white pepper to taste
1 stalk scallion, chopped ⎫
1 tsp sesame oil ⎭ *to garnish*

PROCEDURES:

1. Soak the bean threads in hot water for about 10 minutes. Drain and cut into 3-inch (7.5-cm) lengths.

2. Thaw the fish balls.

TO COOK:

3. Pour the chicken broth into a pot. Add the fish balls and bring to a boil. Turn to low heat and simmer for 5 minutes. Add 1 Tbs fish sauce and salt and pepper to taste.

4. Bring the broth to a boil again and add the soaked bean threads. Turn off heat and garnish with scallion and sesame oil. Serve hot.

NOTE: Once the bean threads have been added, the soup should be served. When left in the broth for a period of time, the bean threads will soak up all the liquid. Therefore this dish can be prepared ahead of time only through step 3. Just before serving, follow step 4 and serve immediately.

Shredded Pork with Bean Threads 豬肉粉絲

As mentioned before, bean threads (or cellophane noodles) are made from mung beans and are therefore highly nutritious. They are a favorite of Chinese cooks because they absorb flavor readily in a simmered dish. Bean threads are also marvelous extenders. For example, if you have some leftover red-cooked poultry or meat, not quite enough to serve alone, add some presoaked bean threads and simmer to get a tasty, substantial dish.

INGREDIENTS:
1 lb (500 g) boneless pork loin or 4 large pork chops
3 Tbs dark soy sauce
1 Tbs Chinese rice wine
¼ tsp sugar   } to marinate shredded pork
¼ tsp salt
1 tsp tapioca starch
4 oz (125 g) bean threads
2 stalks scallions
1 cup chicken broth
3 Tbs peanut or vegetable oil

PROCEDURES:
1. Shred pork into 2-inch-long (5-cm) julienne strips. Marinate in the soy sauce, wine, sugar, salt, and tapioca starch for at least 20 to 30 minutes.

2. Soak the bean threads in warm water for 10 minutes. Drain and cut into 2-inch (5-cm) pieces. Cut scallions into 2-inch (5-cm) pieces.

TO COOK:
3. Heat 3 Tbs oil in a wok over high heat. Add the scallions and stir a few times. Then add the marinated shredded pork and stir for about 2 minutes until the pork changes color. Add the bean threads and mix well with the pork mixture.

4. Pour in 1 cup chicken broth; bring to a boil, cover, turn to medium heat and cook about 4 to 5 minutes or until all the liquid is absorbed. Serve hot.

NOTE: Beef can be used instead of pork. This dish can be covered with aluminum foil and kept warm in the oven for quite a while.

Chinese Cabbage in Cream Sauce 奶油白菜

This beautiful vegetable dish covered with milky white sauce dotted with reddish chopped ham is often served as a banquet dish. Smithfield ham is close in taste, texture, and color to the famous Chinese Kim Hua ham, which is an important ingredient in Chinese cooking. Smithfield ham can be made into a delightful appetizer with the following directions.

Cut the skin and fat from the ham and then simmer the ham over low heat for about 30 minutes. Cut the meat with the grain into 2-inch-wide (5-cm) pieces and place them in a large jar. Dissolve 4 Tbs sugar in 2 cups of boiling water. When cool, add 2 Tbs Chinese rice wine to the sugar solution and pour it over the ham. Cover the jar and refrigerate. This sugar-soaked ham keeps indefinitely. To use the ham as an appetizer, slice the ham, coat with honey, and steam for 20 minutes. This ham makes an exotic appetizer for a formal dinner.

INGREDIENTS:
1¼ lbs (625 g) Chinese cabbage
1½ Tbs tapioca starch
¼ cup milk
3 Tbs peanut or vegetable oil
1 tsp salt
½ tsp sugar
¾ cup chicken broth
2 Tbs Smithfield ham, cooked and finely chopped

PROCEDURES:

1. Separate the cabbage leaves; wash and cut them into 1- by 2½ -inch (2.5- by 6-cm) strips.

2. Combine the tapioca starch and milk in a small bowl; stir until the starch is thoroughly dissolved.

3. Cut off skin and fat of ham. Boil in water for 10 to 15 minutes. When cool, cut off a small piece and chop it into fine pieces; the rest can be saved for other uses.

TO COOK:

4. Heat the oil in the wok over high heat; turn the heat to medium high. Add the cabbage and stir-fry for about 1 minute or until the cabbage strips are thoroughly coated with oil. Add salt and sugar, then pour in the chicken broth and stir well. Bring the stock to a boil; cover the wok and simmer over low heat for 10 minutes. With a strainer, transfer the cabbage to a big plate, and arrange the strips in one direction.

5. Bring the cooking liquid in the wok to a boil. Give the tapioca starch and milk a quick stir to recombine them and add to the wok. Stir until the sauce thickens. Pour it over the cabbage, sprinkle with the chopped ham, and serve at once.

NOTE: This dish can be cooked ahead of time through step 4, simmering the cabbage for 10 minutes. Just before serving, bring the cabbage and liquid to a boil again and then transfer the cabbage with a strainer to a serving plate. Follow step 5 to finish the dish.

Soy Sauce Fish, Shanghai Style 红烧鱼

The Chinese like to eat fish with almost every meal. They consider it rich in protein and iodine and easy to digest, and they feel that their methods of cooking seafood yield more delicate, tastier fish with more aroma and less "fishy" smell than other methods. Fish is usually cooked whole, either steamed, red-cooked, or fried. This eastern-style red-cooked fish has proved to be a very popular family dish.

INGREDIENTS:
1½ lb (750 g) whole fish (sea bass, yellow croaker, whiting, or sea trout)
¾ tsp salt
2 slices ginger root
3 stalks scallions
⅓ cup bamboo shoots, winter
6 to 8 dried Chinese mushrooms
2 Tbs flour
½ cup peanut or vegetable oil
1 Tbs Chinese rice wine
4 Tbs dark soy sauce
2 Tbs rock sugar
¾ cup water

PROCEDURES:
1. Rinse the fish inside and out under cold water; dry completely with paper towels. Slash both sides diagonally in 1½-inch (4-cm) intervals. Rub salt inside and out and set aside for about 10 minutes.

2. Slice ginger root into 1-inch (2.5-cm) slices; cut scallions into 4-inch (10-cm) lengths; slice bamboo shoots into thin round slices. Soak dried mushrooms in hot water for about 15 minutes; when soft, discard stems and cut large mushrooms in halves.

3. Coat both sides of fish with flour.

TO COOK:
4. Heat the wok very hot, add oil and then ginger slices. Gently put in the fish and fry over medium-high heat for 2 to 3 minutes. Turn it carefully and fry the other side until golden brown. Pour off excess oil and add scallions, bamboo shoot slices, mushrooms and then wine, soy sauce, rock sugar, and water. Bring to a boil, cover and cook over low heat for 5 minutes. Remove cover, increase heat, and baste fish until a little more than ½ cup liquid remains. Serve hot or cold but never reheat.

NOTE: Other small whole fish like flounder, striped bass, porgy, or carp can be used.

Sweet and Sour Spareribs 糖醋排骨

This recipe has proved to be very popular with my cooking class students. It can be served either as an hors d'oeuvre or as one of the main dishes. This dish was originally called 4–3–2–1 spareribs by my sister Jane Chao, signifying the ratio of soy sauce (4 portions), sugar (3), vinegar (2), and wine (1). Later on I changed it to 3–3–2–1, as shown in this recipe, and the result is even better because it is less salty. With the ratio 3–3–2–1 in mind, you can easily adjust the recipe to cook for 10 people or even 50 people without having to multiply the number of tablespoons or teaspoons. For instance, to cook 20 pounds (10 kg) of spareribs for a big party, you may use a big soup ladle as a measuring spoon and use 3 soup ladles of soy sauce, 3 soup ladles of sugar, 2 soup ladles of vinegar, and 1 soup ladle of wine to cook the spareribs. The result is equally delicious. Try it!

INGREDIENTS:

1½ lb (750 g) spareribs (ask your butcher to cut across the bones into 1½-inch or
    4-cm sections)
2 slices ginger root
2 stalks scallions
3 to 4 Chinese cabbage leaves
1 Tbs peanut or vegetable oil
4 Tbs dark soy sauce
4 Tbs sugar
2½ Tbs Chin Kiang vinegar
1½ Tbs Chinese rice wine

PROCEDURES:

1. Trim the fat from the spareribs and separate each rib.
2. Slice the ginger root; cut scallions into 2-inch (5-cm) lengths. Shred the Chinese cabbage and place on a serving plate.

TO COOK:

3. Heat the oil in a Dutch oven or a medium-sized pot. Add the ginger slices and scallions. Then add the spareribs and stir-fry about 1 minute to slightly brown them.
4. Add the soy sauce, sugar, vinegar, and wine. Bring to a boil; then cover and simmer over low heat for about 45 minutes. Stir and mix two or three times during that period.
5. Arrange the spareribs on the shredded Chinese cabbage leaves and serve hot.

NOTE: This dish can be prepared ahead of time through step 4 and left in the pot. Warm thoroughly on the stove before serving.

Wonton in Soup 餛飩
(about 60 wontons)

In China, wontons are more often served as snacks or lunch than soup. When served in soup for lunch, shredded roast pork, egg sheets, and presoaked dried mushrooms, in addition to green vegetables, may be added to the soup for color and flavor. Wontons were frequently served by street peddlers, who trotted through the streets of big cities, to the delight of students or people who stayed up late at night. Bubbling hot wontons, served with soup seasoned with dashes of soy sauce, sesame oil, and minced preserved vegetables, were also favorites from the stall-like eating places in the back streets of cities. Simple but versatile, filling but not heavy, easy to cook and serve, wontons are a favorite food with the Chinese.

INGREDIENTS:

1 package (1 lb or 500 g) wonton wrappers
1 lb (500 g) ground pork
1 egg
1 stalk scallion, chopped
1 tsp chopped ginger
3 Tbs dark soy sauce   } filling
1 Tbs Chinese rice wine
½ tsp salt
3 Tbs sesame oil
1 Tbs chicken broth
3 cups chicken broth
2 cups cold water
½ Tbs light soy sauce   } soup
1 Tbs Szechuan preserved vegetable, shredded
½ lb (250 g) bok choy, shredded (use green leaves only)
2 stalks scallions, chopped   } to garnish soup
1 Tbs sesame oil

PROCEDURES:

1. Thaw the wonton wrappers. Then open the package and cover the wrappers with a damp towel for about 20 minutes before using.

2. Mix the ground pork with the egg, scallion, ginger, soy sauce, wine, salt, sesame oil, and chicken broth to make the filling.

3. Put ½ tsp of filling in the center of each wrapper. Moisten the edges of the wrapper with some water and fold over at the center. Gently press the edges together. Fold in half again lengthwise and then pull the corners one over the other and press them together with a little water. A properly wrapped wonton resembles a nurse's cap.

TO COOK:

4. Boil 4 quarts of water in a deep pot or in the wok. Add the wontons to the boiling water and bring to a boil. Add 1 cup cold water and again bring to a

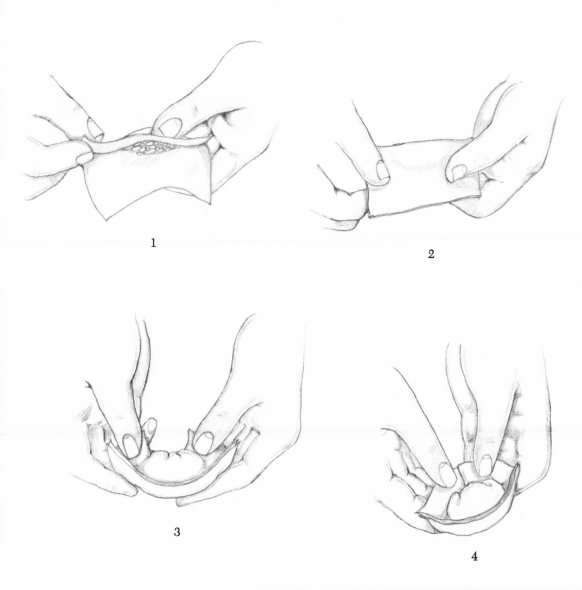

1

2

3

4

boil. Repeat the process twice, each time adding 1 cup cold water and bringing the pot to a boil. When wontons float to the surface again, they are ready. Use a strainer to dish out 5 or 6 wontons into each soup bowl.

5. Heat 3 cups of chicken broth with 2 cups cold water. Add the soy sauce, Szechuan preserved vegetable, and bok choy pieces and cook for about 1 minute. Garnish with chopped scallions and sesame oil. Ladle the soup with some bok choy shreds into each bowl so that the wontons float up. Serve hot.

NOTE: Wontons can be made weeks ahead of time and frozen before cooking. No need to defrost before cooking. After being cooked, leftover wontons can be pan-fried in a pan with a nonstick finish for a few minutes on each side. These crispy wontons make excellent hors d'oeuvres or snacks. Diced uncooked shrimp can be added to the filling before wrapping.

Lion's Head 獅子頭

Chinese people like to use words like "dragon," "phoenix," or "lion" to describe high-quality products. In Imperial China, the dragon and phoenix symbolized emperors and empresses; and since the lion is the king of the jungle, to use its name implies both high quality and large size. In this dish, the Lion's Head is actually a large meatball, sitting on a bed of cabbage which symbolizes the lion's mane.

This is a famous dish from Yangchow, in Eastern China. Traditionally it is served on New Year's Day, although it can be served at other times of the year. If it is served on New Year's Day, four meatballs should be made to symbolize the four blessings: luck, prosperity, longevity, and happiness.

INGREDIENTS:
1 lb (500 g) ground pork
3 Tbs dark soy sauce
1 Tbs Chinese rice wine
1 stalk scallion, finely chopped
1 tsp finely chopped ginger root
4 fresh water chestnuts, peeled and chopped
1 egg, lightly beaten
4 Tbs tapioca starch, dissolved in 8 Tbs chicken broth
1 lb (50 g) Chinese cabbage
2 Tbs peanut or vegetable oil
½ tsp sugar
½ cup chicken broth
1 Tbs tapioca starch dissolved in 2 Tbs cold water

PROCEDURES:
1. Mix the ground pork with 2 Tbs of the soy sauce, the wine, scallion, ginger, water chestnuts, egg, and 1 Tbs of the tapioca starch—chicken broth mixture. Shape the meat mixture into 4 to 6 balls. Set aside.

2. Wash the Chinese cabbage. Cut each stalk in half lengthwise, then slice the pieces crosswise at 3-inch (7.5-cm) intervals. Arrange the cabbage in a layer on the bottom of a heavy 2- to 3-quart ovenproof casserole or large pot.

TO COOK:
3. Heat the oil in a wok. Give the remaining tapioca starch-chicken broth mixture a quick stir to recombine it. Dip the meatballs into the tapioca starch, coating them thoroughly and brown them in the wok; turn only once.

4. Gently remove the meatballs from the wok and place them on the bed of cabbage in the casserole. Add sugar, the remaining 1 Tbs of soy sauce, and chicken

broth and bring to a boil. Then cover the casserole tightly, reduce to low heat and simmer for about an hour.

5. Arrange the cabbage on a platter with the meatballs on top. Thicken the sauce by adding 1 Tbs tapioca starch mixed with 2 Tbs water. Pour the gravy over the meatballs. Serve hot.

NOTE: Lion's Head can be made several hours before serving and simply reheated on top of the stove.

For those who prefer not to eat pork, ground beef or veal can be used as a substitute.

Sweet and Sour Squid　糖醋墨鱼

This beautiful, delicate-tasting dish is served as one of the main dishes. The tender white squid is embellished with green pepper or snow peas, black tree ears, and slices of white water chestnuts.

INGREDIENTS:

1 lb (500 g) fresh squid
½ tsp salt
1 tsp tapioca starch } to marinate squid
1 Tbs Chinese rice wine
2 Tbs tree ears (before soaking)
2 green peppers or ¼ lb (125 g) snow peas (parboiled)
6 to 8 fresh water chestnuts
2 slices ginger root
1 stalk scallion, cut into ½-inch (1½-cm) pieces
½ Tbs garlic, chopped
2 Tbs light soy sauce
3 Tbs sugar
2 Tbs Chin Kiang vinegar } combined seasoning sauce
2 Tbs Chinese rice wine
½ Tbs tapioca starch
1 tsp sesame oil
4 Tbs peanut or vegetable oil

PROCEDURES:

1. Remove the head and tentacles of the squid; save for another use. Cut the squid open carefully to become one flat piece. Remove the membrane and cartilage and rinse in cold water. Score the inside crosswise and then diagonally into a crisscross pattern; then cut into 2-inch (5-cm) pieces. Marinate with salt, tapioca starch, and wine for about 15 minutes.

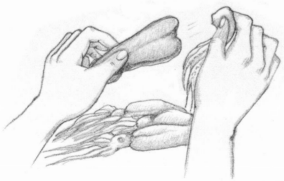

1. Remove the head and tentacles.

2. Remove the membrane . . .

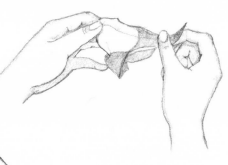

3. . . . and cartilage.

4. Score the inside crosswise.

2. Soak the tree ears in hot water for about 20 minutes. Drain and put aside.

3. Cut the green pepper into 1-inch (2.5-cm) pieces; peel and slice the water chestnuts.

4. Combine soy sauce, sugar, vinegar, wine, tapioca starch, and sesame oil to make the seasoning sauce.

TO COOK:

5. Heat 2 Tbs oil in wok. First drop in the ginger slices, then the squid. Stir-fry over high heat until done, about 2 minutes. Remove and set aside.

6. Heat another 2 Tbs oil to sauté scallion and garlic, then add tree ears, water chestnut slices, and green pepper, finally stirring in the seasoning sauce. Stir until well mixed. Then add squid and mix well. Serve hot.

NOTE: Once the preparations are done, the cooking takes only 2 to 3 minutes. This dish has best results when served as a last-minute stir-fried dish.

Stir-Fried Rice Noodles
with Shrimps and Vegetables　蝦仁炒米粉

This dish is an Amoy specialty, although it is served in other areas as well. Light and absorbent, the rice noodles are excellent for stir-frying and blend wonderfully with the firm pink shrimps and crisp green cabbage. In China this dish is often served as a snack or lunch dish. It is also excellent for buffet dinners.

INGREDIENTS:
½ lb (250 g) rice noodles
½ lb (250 g) raw shrimps, peeled and deveined
1 Tbs Chinese rice wine ⎫
½ tsp salt　　　　　　　 ⎬ to marinate shrimp
½ Tbs tapioca starch 　 ⎭
4 Tbs peanut or vegetable oil
2 stalks scallions, shredded
3 cups Chinese cabbage, shredded
1 tsp salt
½ tsp sugar
1½ Tbs light soy sauce
½ cup chicken broth

PROCEDURES:
1. Rinse shrimps with cold water. Drain and pat dry thoroughly with paper towels. Marinate the shrimps with wine, ½ tsp salt, and tapioca starch.
2. Soak the rice noodles in hot water for 10 to 15 minutes until soft; drain well.

TO COOK:
3. Heat a wok over high heat until hot. Add 2 Tbs oil and stir-fry the shrimps for 1 minute or until they change color. Remove and set on a plate.
4. Heat the wok with remaining 2 Tbs oil. Stir-fry the scallions and cabbage for ½ minute, then add 1 tsp salt, sugar, and the soaked rice noodles, and keep stirring for 1 more minute. Add the soy sauce and chicken broth. Turn the heat to high and stir-fry until all the liquid is absorbed. Add the cooked shrimps and mix well. Serve hot.

NOTE: Covered with aluminum foil, this dish can be kept warm in the oven for about ½ hour. Uncooked rice noodles, like cellophane noodles (bean threads), can be deep-fried in very hot oil (about 400° F or 204° C) for about 2 seconds. They will puff up immediately and can be used as a decorative base for dishes that do not have sauces.

Cold Noodle Salad with Sesame Paste Sauce 芝麻醬涼拌麵

Many of my students have been surprised and delighted by this cold noodle dish. It is a highly popular picnic fare and is excellent for other summer meals. Furthermore, it gives you a chance to use some interesting serving dishes. The cooked meat, cucumbers, egg shreds, and cold noodles can be served in separate dishes so that each person can mix according to individual taste.

INGREDIENTS:

1 lb (500 g) fresh egg noodles
2 Tbs sesame oil
1 Tbs dark soy sauce
½ lb (250 g) frozen, precooked roast pork
1 cucumber
2 eggs
pinch of salt
a little peanut or vegetable oil
2 Tbs sesame paste, diluted with 3 Tbs warm water ⎫
½ tsp salt
2 tsp sugar
2 Tbs dark soy sauce
1 Tbs white rice vinegar ⎬ sauce
2 tsp hot oil (chili oil)
2 cloves garlic, finely chopped
2 stalks scallions, finely chopped ⎭

PROCEDURES:

1. Drop the noodles in boiling water and boil 4 to 5 minutes. Rinse under cold water and drain thoroughly. Add 2 Tbs sesame oil and 1 Tbs dark soy sauce to the noodles and toss well. Cover and chill in the refrigerator.

2. Thaw the roast pork and shred into 2-inch-long (5-cm) strips. Peel and shred the cucumber.

3. Beat the eggs with a pinch of salt and set aside for 10 minutes. Heat a little oil in a wok, pour in ¼ of the beaten egg and make an egg sheet by swirling egg onto sides of wok. Lift up and flip over and let cook briefly on the other side. Repeat procedure to make 3 more sheets. Let the egg sheets cool, then shred them into 2-inch-long (5-cm) strips.

4. Mix the remaining ingredients to make the combined sesame paste sauce. When it is time to serve, pour the sauce all over the noodles and toss well. Transfer onto a large platter. Top with the shredded cucumber, roast pork, and egg strips and serve.

NOTE: Cooked cold chicken, shredded, can also be added to this dish. Bean sprouts and shredded Chinese cabbage can be used instead of cucumbers. This dish is served both in the eastern and western regions of China. When served in the eastern area, hot oil is either omitted or used very sparingly.

Spiced Pork 醬肉

The Chinese name for this dish is actually "bean sauce meat" because the pork has been marinated with sweet bean sauce and then cooked in dark soy sauce and rock sugar. It is not a "spicy" dish at all as the name seems to indicate. This is a favorite dish for Chinese and Americans alike, and one of my cooking class students even served this dish in a cafeteria and found it well received by everyone.

Rock sugar is much more nutritious than white refined sugar. It is often used in Chinese cooking to make the sauce thick and to add a glaze to the gravy.

INGREDIENTS:
1½ lbs (750 g) fresh ham or boneless pork
3 Tbs sweet bean sauce
3 Tbs dark soy sauce
1 Tbs Chinese rice wine
1 whole star anise
¼ cup rock sugar

PROCEDURES:
1. Wash the pork; wipe dry. Then rub all sides with sweet bean paste and marinate at least 2 to 3 hours in the refrigerator.

TO COOK:
2. Place the soy sauce, wine, and star anise in a deep pot and bring to a boil, then add the pork and 1 cup boiling water. Simmer over low heat for ½ hour. Then add the rock sugar and continue to simmer 1 hour more, turning the meat frequently.

3. When the sauce has been reduced to ½ cup and is rather thick, remove pot from the heat and let meat cool in the pot.

4. Slice the pork and arrange it attractively on a plate. Pour the thick dark sauce on top.

NOTE: This dish is excellent for buffet dinners or large parties since it can be done totally ahead of time and served at room temperature. Veal can be used instead of pork.

Meat Platter in Three Colors 炒三練

Unusually pretty, this dish is excellent for entertaining and even banquets. The long and lean white chicken shreds contrast beautifully with the crisp green shredded snow peas and reddish brown shredded beef in hoisin sauce.

INGREDIENTS:
1 whole chicken breast, skinned and boned
1 Tbs Chinese rice wine ⎫
1 tsp salt ⎪
½ tsp sugar ⎬ to marinate shredded chicken
1 egg white ⎪
1 tsp minced ginger ⎭
¾ lb (375 g) flank steak or any steak
1 Tbs dark soy sauce ⎫
1 Tbs Chinese rice wine ⎪
2 tsp hoisin sauce ⎬ to marinate shredded beef
1 tsp sugar ⎪
2 tsp tapioca starch ⎭
½ lb (250 g) fresh snow peas
5 Tbs peanut or vegetable oil
½ tsp salt
¼ tsp sugar

PROCEDURES:
1. Shred the chicken breast into 2-inch-long (5-cm) julienne strips. This should yield 1½ cups of meat. Mix the wine, salt, sugar, egg white, and ginger and marinate the chicken in this mixture for at least 20 to 30 minutes.

2. Shred the beef and marinate for 20 to 30 minutes in soy sauce, wine, hoisin sauce, sugar, and tapioca starch.

3. Rinse and then shred the snow peas. Set aside.

TO COOK:
4. Heat 1 Tbs oil in wok. Stir-fry shredded snow peas until coated with oil. Add ½ tsp salt and ¼ tsp sugar; stir and mix well for about 1 minute. Remove and place snow peas in the center of a serving platter.

5. Heat 2 Tbs oil in wok. Add the marinated chicken and stir over high heat for about 2 minutes or until the chicken turns white. Remove and place on one end of the platter.

6. Heat another 2 Tbs oil over high heat. Add marinated beef and stir-fry for about 2 minutes or until the beef loses its redness. Remove and place on the other end of the platter. Serve hot.

NOTE: The cutting and marinating can be done ahead of time (even overnight) and the food refrigerated. The final stir-frying takes only a few minutes. Fine shredding is important to make this dish pretty. It will be easier to slice and then shred if you first partially freeze the meat for a while to make it firmer.

Yangchow Fried Rice 揚州炒飯

Yangchow Fried Rice is the fanciest and most elegant fried rice dish. To the surprise of many Americans who are familiar with the Cantonese style fried rice, no soy sauce is used in this delicate dish. Instead, the beautiful fluffy white rice is embellished with green peas, reddish roast pork and ham, pink shrimp, light yellow bamboo shoots, dark brown dried mushrooms, yellow eggs, and the crunchy white fresh water chestnuts. It is a favorite fried rice dish for family members and excellent for entertaining guests.

INGREDIENTS:
½ lb (250 g) Smithfield ham
½ lb (250 g) peeled and deveined frozen shrimps
2 tsp Chinese rice wine ⎫
1 tsp tapioca starch ⎬ *to marinate shrimp*
½ tsp salt ⎭
6 dried mushrooms
¼ lb (125 g) precooked roast pork
½ cup bamboo shoots
½ lb (250 g) fresh snow peas or frozen green peas
6 to 8 fresh water chestnuts
6 Tbs peanut or vegetable oil
2 eggs beaten with a dash of salt
3 stalks scallion, chopped
4 cups cooked rice
1 tsp salt
dash of white pepper

PROCEDURES:
1. Cut off skin and fat of Smithfield ham. Boil the ham in water for about 15 minutes. Dice ham when cool.

2. Defrost shrimp and then rinse with cold water. Pat completely dry with paper towels. Marinate in wine, tapioca starch, and salt for at least 15 minutes.

3. Soak the mushrooms in boiling hot water for about 15 minutes. Cut off and remove stems. Dice mushrooms.

4. Dice the roast pork, then dice the bamboo shoots. Parboil the snow peas in boiling water. After rinsing with cold water, cut into small pieces. Peel and then dice the water chestnuts.

TO COOK:
5. Heat 1 Tbs oil in wok. Scramble the eggs and break into small pieces until quite dry. Remove and set aside.

6. Add another 1 Tbs oil to wok Stir-fry the marinated shrimp for about 1 minute or until they change color. Remove and set aside.

7. With another 2 Tbs oil, sauté scallions, mushrooms, ham, roast pork, bamboo shoots, water chestnuts, and snow peas for about 1 minute. Remove to a plate.

8. Heat 2 Tbs oil in wok; add rice and stir well until rice is coated with oil. Add 1 tsp salt and dash of pepper; mix well. Mix in the scrambled eggs and then the cooked shrimp, mushrooms, ham, roast pork, bamboo shoots, water chestnuts, and snow peas. Stir well. Serve hot.

NOTE: This dish can be covered with aluminum foil and kept warm in the oven for about half an hour. It can also be cooked completely ahead of time and warmed up by stir-frying thoroughly in the wok over high heat.

Stir-Fried Rice Cakes (New Year's Cakes) 什錦炒年糕
with Six Kinds of Delicacies

This rice cake dish is a must for the Chinese New Year dinner or lunch, although it can be served at other times as well. New Year's rice cakes (or *Nien Gao*) have special connotations, because "Nien" means "year," and "Gao" (cake) has the same sound as the word for "high" or "tall," symbolizing moving up higher and higher in position or career in the coming year. Most Americans have never had this famous dish, and to the surprise of many of my cooking class students, they find it delicious, delicate, and fun to eat. They even nicknamed the white rice cake slices as "mini tongue depressors" because of their similarity in shape and look. It is also an excellent one-dish meal and can be served for lunch, snack, or buffet dinners.

The "red-in-snow" used in this dish is a delicious green preserved vegetable. It is often used as a seasoning in stir-fried dishes because it is remarkably refreshing and crisp and adds flavor to other ingredients. The name comes from its red roots, which become visible in the snow in early spring.

INGREDIENTS:
1 lb (500 g) sliced dried rice cakes
6 dried mushrooms
¼ lb (125 g) peeled and deveined frozen shrimps
1 tsp Chinese rice wine ⎫
¼ tsp salt ⎬ to marinate shrimp
1 tsp tapioca starch ⎭
1 cup lean pork, shredded
1 Tbs dark soy sauce ⎫
1 Tbs Chinese rice wine ⎪
½ tsp sugar ⎬ to marinate shredded pork
1 tsp tapioca starch ⎭
½ cup bamboo shoots, shredded
3 cups Chinese cabbage, shredded
6 Tbs peanut or vegetable oil
1 tsp salt
¼ cup red-in-snow preserved vegetables, chopped
2 Tbs dark soy sauce
⅓ cup chicken broth

PROCEDURES:
1. Soak the dried rice cake slices in cold water overnight or at least 12 hours. Drain before cooking.

2. Soak the mushrooms in hot water until soft. Discard stems and shred the mushrooms.

3. Defrost and rinse the raw shrimp. Pat dry thoroughly with paper towels. Marinate with wine, salt, and tapioca starch.

4. Marinate the pork with soy sauce, wine, sugar, and tapioca starch.

TO COOK:

5. Heat a wok very hot. Add 2 Tbs oil and stir-fry the shrimps for about 1 minute. Remove and set aside.

6. Add another 2 Tbs oil to wok. Stir-fry the shredded pork until the color changes (about 1 minute). Add mushrooms, mix well and set aside.

7. Heat 2 Tbs oil in same wok. Stir-fry the bamboo shoots and Chinese cabbage for 1 minute. Add 1 tsp salt and mix well. Put back the pork mixture. Add the chopped red-in-snow and cook together for 1 minute.

8. Add the drained rice cake slices and sprinkle dark soy sauce and chicken broth on the rice cakes. Stir with the meat mixture until the cake slices are limp. Finally mix in the cooked shrimp and serve hot.

NOTE: Four or five pieces of fresh rice cake may be used instead of the dried cakes and shredded beef or chicken may be used instead of pork. Fresh rice cakes must be soaked and sliced before use. This dish can be covered with aluminum foil and kept warm in the oven for about half an hour.

Deep-Fried Shrimp Balls 炸蝦球

Since shrimps are generally quite expensive, this is considered a high-quality, banquet-style dish. In China it is often served as one of the main courses when entertaining. But because of their small size and delicate taste, the shrimp balls are also excellent hors d'oeuvres.

INGREDIENTS:

1 lb (500 g) peeled and deveined raw shrimp
2 egg whites
3 oz (90 g) ground pork fat or blanched fatty bacon
1 Tbs tapioca starch
1 tsp salt
⅛ tsp white pepper
1 Tbs Chinese rice wine
one ½-inch (1-cm) piece fresh ginger root
2 cups peanut or vegetable oil
2 Tbs Szechuan peppercorn } to make the flavored peppercorn-salt as dip
¼ cup salt or coarse salt

PROCEDURES:

1. Use a cleaver or a food processor to chop the raw shrimps into a fine paste.

2. Beat the egg whites until foamy; add the ground pork fat and beat together for about 2 minutes. Add the ground shrimp, tapioca starch, salt, pepper, and wine. Squeeze out the ginger juice into the shrimp mixture with a garlic press. Mix well. (This shrimp paste can be kept covered in the refrigerator for a few hours or overnight.)

TO COOK:

3. Heat a wok very hot. Add oil and heat over medium heat. With your left hand, take a handful of the shrimp paste and squeeze your fingers into a fist. A ball about the size of a walnut will spurt from between your thumb and forefinger. With your right hand, use a measuring tablespoon dipped in cold water (to prevent sticking) to scoop up the shrimp ball and drop it into the hot oil. Repeat until you have made all the balls. Fry about 2 minutes or until they float to the top and become fluffy. Turn the balls to fry evenly. Do not overcook (overfrying will shrink the shrimp balls). Transfer the balls to a paper-lined plate to drain. Serve hot with peppercorn-salt.

4. To make the peppercorn-salt, heat salt and Szechuan peppercorn in a dry pan over low heat. Stir until the salt is brown and the peppercorn is dark and smells good. Let cool, then crush with the wooden handle of the cleaver or grind in a blender. Strain through a fine sieve. This keeps well in a tightly covered bottle.

NOTE: The shrimp balls can be frozen and reheated in a preheated 350° F (177° C) oven.

Red-Cooked Duck 紅燒鴨

Because it can be done ahead of time, this Shanghai-style duck is good not only for family meals but also for entertaining. The tender, delicate duck meat served with a tasty delicious glazed sauce goes very well with the Peking steamed buns or plain rice. This is a favorite duck dish with almost all of my cooking class students.

INGREDIENTS:
4 to 5 lb (2 kg) fresh or frozen duck
1 tsp salt
6 Tbs dark soy sauce
¼ cup Chinese rice wine
1 whole star anise
2 stalks scallions, cut into 2-inch (5-cm) lengths
2 slices ginger root
¼ cup rock sugar
4 cups water
2 tsp sesame oil

PROCEDURES:

1. Remove extra fat from body of duck. Rinse duck with water, drain and dry well. Rub salt inside the duck and brush 1 Tbs of the soy sauce onto the duck. Let stand in a large pot for 1 hour.

TO COOK:

2. Preheat oven to 400° F (204° C). Put the duck breast side up on an oiled roasting rack and place over a broiler pan filled with 1 inch (2.5 cm) of water. Roast the duck until the skin is browned, about 30 minutes.

3. Add 5 Tbs soy sauce, wine, star anise, scallions, ginger, rock sugar, and water to the large pot. Bring to a boil, then put in the roasted duck, breast side down, giblets, and neck (with the skin removed). Boil for 5 minutes. Cover and turn heat to medium-low and cook for 1 hour. Turn the duck over and continue cooking for 1 hour or until the duck is very tender. Baste with the sauce a few times.

4. Carefully take the whole duck out and lay it on a large platter, breast side up. Keep warm in oven. Discard the star anise and ginger and skim the fat off the sauce. Add sesame oil, mix well, and then pour the liquid onto the duck. (If there is too much liquid, boil it down to about ¾ cup.) Serve hot.

NOTE: This duck can be cooked ahead of time through step 3. Before serving just warm up the duck by simmering it on the stove and then follow step 4 to finish and serve the dish.

Quail Eggs in Brown Sauce 紅扒鶴蛋

A fancy vegetable dish, this is often considered banquet fare by vegetarians and monks. The golden brown tiny quail eggs mixed with umbrella-shaped straw mushrooms and delicious yellow baby corn surrounded by crispy green snow peas is a delight to look at. Quail eggs (usually cooked, shelled, and stored in the can), although unfamiliar to most Americans, have a delicate taste. They are often used in fancy vegetable dishes or in soup.

INGREDIENTS:
one 15-oz (500-g) can quail eggs
2 Tbs dark soy sauce
1 tsp sugar
1 tsp salt } *combined seasoning sauce*
1 Tbs tapioca starch
½ cup chicken broth
1 tsp sesame oil
½ lb (250 g) fresh snow peas
2 Tbs flour
1½ cups peanut or vegetable oil for deep-frying
3 Tbs peanut or vegetable oil for stir-frying
one 15-oz (500-g) can straw mushrooms
one 15-oz (500-g) can baby corn

PROCEDURES:

1. Marinate the quail eggs in 2 Tbs soy sauce for about 10 minutes, turning the eggs frequently. Remove quail eggs and set aside. Save the soy sauce.

2. Add sugar, salt, tapioca starch, chicken broth, and sesame oil to the soy sauce used to marinate the eggs. This is the seasoning sauce.

3. Rinse the snow peas and parboil.

TO COOK:

4. Coat the quail eggs with flour; heat the oil in a wok and deep-fry the eggs until golden brown. Set aside.

5. Heat 1 Tbs oil in the wok; stir-fry the snow peas for a few seconds. Add half of the seasoning sauce and continue to stir-fry for about 1 minute. Remove to plate and arrange attractively around outer edge.

6. Heat another 2 Tbs oil in the wok; stir-fry the straw mushrooms and baby corn for about 1 minute. Add the remaining seasoning sauce and mix thoroughly. Add quail eggs and stir well; pour in the middle of the plate. Serve hot.

NOTE: The quail eggs, after being coated with flour and deep-fried until golden brown, can be served as hors d'oeuvres.

Three Kinds of Shredded Delicacy Soup 扣三絲湯

White shredded chicken, red Smithfield ham, and green snow peas give this banquet-style soup its beautiful coloring. Egg strips can also be used to add a yellow accent. The custom is to first let your guests see the beautiful design before you mix up the ingredients and serve.

INGREDIENTS:
½ lb (250 g) Smithfield ham
1 whole chicken breast, uncooked, with skin and bone removed
8 cups water
2 stalks scallion, cut into 2-inch (5-cm) pieces
3 slices ginger root
¼ lb (125 g) fresh snow peas
1 cup bamboo shoots
1 dried Chinese mushroom
2 tsp salt

PROCEDURES:
1. Remove skin and fat from ham. Boil the ham and chicken breast in 8 cups of water with scallion and ginger for about 20 minutes. Remove the ham and chicken; let cool. Save 6 cups of the soup stock for later use. Cut the cold ham into thin strips and tear the cold chicken into shreds.

2. Shred the snow peas and bamboo shoots. Soak the mushroom in hot water for 15 minutes, then remove the stem.

TO COOK:
3. Place the mushroom stem side up in the center of a medium-sized bowl. Arrange the shredded chicken, ham, and snow peas attractively around the mushroom at the bottom of bowl. Add bamboo shoot strips to fill the center. Sprinkle on 1 tsp salt, then pour in ½ cup soup stock. Steam for 20 minutes.

4. In a separate saucepan bring the remaining 5½ cups soup stock to a boil and add 1 tsp salt.

5. Put the steamed bowl upside down in a large soup tureen. Without removing the steamed bowl, pour the boiling soup stock around the bowl. Then remove the steamed bowl and serve.

Scallops and Chinese Radish Balls 干貝蘿蔔球

For those who have never had Chinese radishes, this recipe offers a pleasant introduction. This light vegetable dish has a refreshing taste. The round radish balls acquire a translucent look after being boiled and soaked in cold water. They are lovely to look at surrounded by the white glazed sauce and the yellow scallop shreds. Chinese radishes are also excellent for soups. They combine especially well with Smithfield ham in soup.

INGREDIENTS:
1½ oz (45 g) dried scallops
1½ cups chicken broth
2 Chinese radish, about 2 lbs (1 kg)
1 slice ginger
1 Tbs Chinese rice wine
½ tsp salt
1 Tbs tapioca starch dissolved in 1½ Tbs water
2 Tbs peanut or vegetable oil

PROCEDURES:

1. Soak the dried scallops in ½ cup boiling hot chicken broth for about ½ hour. Steam with broth for about ½ hour. When cool, shred the scallops with fingers. Save the stock for later use.

2. Use a melon ball scoop to cut the radish into 30 small balls. Boil the radish balls in water for about 10 minutes; drain and soak in cold water.

TO COOK:

3. Heat 2 Tbs oil in wok; stir-fry the ginger slice and radish balls for a few seconds. Add rice wine, salt, shredded scallops with stock, and 1 cup chicken broth. Cook over low heat for 1 minute. Thicken with tapioca starch mixture. Serve hot.

NOTE: Dried scallops are very tasty and expensive, but a little goes a long way. Dried shrimps can be used instead of dried scallops. Soak the dried shrimp in ½ cup of boiling hot chicken broth for ½ hour and then steam them for another ½ hour before use. Do not shred or cut the shrimps.

The preparation for this dish can be done ahead of time through step 2. The final step takes but a few minutes.

Sautéed Mixed Vegetables 什錦素會

This is a fancy vegetable dish, often served at banquets. It is not only a joy to look at with its great variety of colors, but also marvelous to taste. The roll-cut method called for here exposes many more surfaces of the vegetables than do other cutting techniques. Although considered a banquet dish, Sautéed Mixed Vegetables is quite simple to make. This is a favorite dish with many Americans and Chinese alike.

INGREDIENTS:

1 Chinese radish (about ½ lb or 250 g)
1 carrot
½ cup winter bamboo shoots
10 ears of baby corn
¼ lb (125 g) fresh snow peas
6 dried Chinese mushrooms
2 oz (60 g) dried bean curd slices
3 Tbs peanut or vegetable oil
½ can (7½ oz or 225 g) straw mushrooms
12 quail eggs
3 Tbs light soy sauce
½ tsp salt
½ tsp sugar
⅔ cup chicken broth
1 Tbs sesame oil
2 Tbs tapioca starch dissolved in 2 Tbs cold water

PROCEDURES:

1. Roll-cut the radish, carrot, bamboo shoots, and baby corn into small varied shapes. Place them in boiling water and boil for about 2 minutes (the radish and carrot should be put in first). Rinse with cold water. Parboil the snow peas for ½ minute, then rinse in cold water.

2. Soak the Chinese mushrooms and dried bean curd slices in hot water in separate bowls for about 20 minutes. Cut off and discard stems of mushrooms and cut into smaller sizes. Cut the dried bean curd slices into smaller pieces.

TO COOK:

3. Heat 3 Tbs oil in wok. Stir-fry the black mushrooms and straw mushrooms for a few seconds. Then add all the vegetables (radish, carrots, bamboo shoots, baby corn, and snow peas), the dried bean curd, and the quail eggs. Mix well; then add soy sauce, salt, sugar, and chicken broth. Stir over high heat for about 2 minutes.

4. Thicken with the tapioca starch mixture. Garnish with sesame oil and serve.

NOTE: Once the preparations are done (the first two steps), the cooking takes only a few minutes. But do put all the parboiled vegetables together on one plate with the dried bean curd slices and quail eggs. The soy sauce, salt, sugar, and chicken broth can also be assembled in a small bowl. For instructions on roll-cutting, see Basic Cutting Techniques, page 188.

Stuffed Winter Melon with Ham　火腿冬瓜夹

Winter melon, used primarily in soups, is considered to have medicinal value by the Chinese. When they do not feel well, they drink winter melon soup. Here the translucent winter melon, stuffed with reddish ham and saturated with a thick, glazed sauce, becomes an elegant main dish. It is so delicate that it literally melts in your mouth.

INGREDIENTS:
2 lbs (1 kg) winter melon slice
½ lb (250 g) ground pork
1 stalk scallion, finely chopped
1 Tbs ginger juice
1 tsp salt
1 tsp Chinese rice wine ⎫ to marinate pork
2 tsp tapioca starch
1 tsp sesame oil
¼ tsp white pepper
½ lb (250 g) Smithfield ham
½ cup chicken broth
⅛ tsp salt
¼ tsp white pepper
2 tsp tapioca starch dissolved in 2 Tbs water

PROCEDURES:
1. Peel the skin and discard the seeds from the winter melon slice. Cut into double slices 1 inch (2.5 cm) wide, 1½ inches (4 cm) long, and ⅓ inch (8 mm) thick.

2. Mix the ground pork with the marinade ingredients listed above. Stir in one direction.

3. Cut the ham into 20 long, thin slices measuring ½ inch (1.5 cm) wide and 1½ inches (4 cm) long (the ham does not have to be cooked first).

4. Put ½ Tbs of the pork mixture and one slice of ham into each double slice of winter melon. (The ham should be on top of the pork mixture.) Arrange all the stuffed winter melon (stuffed side down) in a shallow bowl.

TO COOK:

5. Add ½ cup chicken broth to the bowl. Put the bowl in a steamer and steam 20 minutes. Strain and save the broth from the bowl.

6. Turn the bowl with the drained stuffed winter melon upside down on a serving platter. Bring the broth to a boil in a wok or sauce pan. Season with ⅛ tsp salt and ¼ tsp pepper to taste. Stir in the tapioca starch mixture until broth thickens. Pour it over the winter melon. Serve hot.

NOTE: Since this dish uses a steamer, you can use the wok to cook other dishes. The melon can be stuffed and arranged nicely in the shallow bowl and refrigerated. Half an hour before serving, just follow step 5, put the bowl in the steamer and steam 20 minutes. Prepare the sauce as in step 6 and pour over the stuffed melon and serve.

Smoked Fish, Soochow Style 蘇式燻魚

Smoked fish is usually served in the first course of a banquet as one of the ingredients in the assorted cold platter. It can also be served alone as one of the main dishes. With the new improved method illustrated here, no smoking is needed, and yet the fish acquires the same dark-brown color; it is even more succulent and flavorful than fish smoked in the traditional way.

INGREDIENTS:

2 lb (1 kg) cod steak, carp, or sea bass (ask the fish dealer to cut the whole fish into steak slices ½-inch or 1.5-cm wide)

5 Tbs dark soy sauce
1 Tbs Chinese rice wine
3 stalks scallions, cut into 2-inch-long lengths   } to marinate fish
5 slices ginger root
4 Tbs sugar
1 tsp five-spice powder
1 cup boiling water
2 cups peanut or vegetable oil
1 Tbs sesame oil

PROCEDURES:

1. Rinse the fish, drain, and dry thoroughly with paper towels. Cut large fish pieces in half. Marinate in the soy sauce, wine, scallions, and ginger root for 4 to 5 hours or overnight.

2. Dissolve the sugar and five-spice powder in 1 cup boiling water. Set aside near the stove.

TO COOK:

3. Remove the marinated fish to a colander to drain. Heat the 2 cups of oil in a wok over high heat until very hot, then turn to medium heat. Put 2 or 3 pieces of fish at a time in the oil (do not crowd them), and fry one side at a time for about 4 to 5 minutes. Turn the fish over and fry the other side until dark brown. Remove and set aside.

4. Remove all the oil from the wok. Pour the soy sauce mixture used to marinate the fish into the wok. Add the sugar, five-spice powder, and water mixture, then add 1 Tbs sesame oil. Heat to a boil. Put the drained fish, a few at a time, in this liquid and cook for about 3 minutes; turn over and cook for another ½ minute. Remove to plate. When cold, cut into smaller pieces and serve. Serve cold.

NOTE: The cooked fish can be kept in a covered container for weeks in the refrigerator and for months in the freezer.

Fish Wrapped in Dried Bean Curd Sheet Rolls 腐衣黄鱼

This dish originated in Ningpo, on the eastern seacoast of China where fish is the staple food. These fish fillets wrapped in dried bean curd sheets (*fu yi*) are especially nutritious. The sheets are made from soybean milk, which is high in protein and vitamins. When bean milk is boiled, a film forms on top of the liquid, much as with regular milk. This film is lifted off and dried. It usually comes in large half-moon-shaped sheets which are wrapped in paper. Since *fu yi* is very brittle, it should be handled with care.

INGREDIENTS:

½ lb (250 g) fillet of sole, pike, or flounder ⎫
½ tsp salt
¼ tsp sugar   ⎬ filling
dash white pepper
1 tsp Chinese rice wine   ⎭
6 pieces dried bean curd skin
½ egg, lightly beaten ⎫
2 Tbs flour
¼ tsp salt   ⎬ to make thin paste
2 tsp minced scallion
3 Tbs cold water   ⎭
2 cups peanut or vegetable oil
2 Tbs Szechuan peppercorn ⎫
                          ⎬ to make peppercorn-salt dip
¼ cup salt or coarse salt ⎭

PROCEDURES:

1. Cut the fillet into 1½-inch-long (4-cm) julienne strips. Combine the cut fish with the rest of the filling ingredients and mix. Refrigerate for 30 minutes.

2. Handling the dried bean curd skin carefully, place each sheet between damp cloths. Set aside for 15 to 20 minutes or until they are soft enough to handle. (Sprinkle water on them if necessary to make them soft sooner.)

3. Mix the egg, flour, salt, scallion, and water all together to form a thin paste. Set aside.

4. Brush each skin lightly with the paste. Loosely stack the skins in two piles of three so that each rounded edge extends 2 inches (5 cm) beyond the next one. Divide the fish filling into 2 portions. Take one portion of filling and place it along the straight side of the bean curd skin. Loosely cover the filling with the straight side of the bean curd skin, tuck in both ends, and roll until the skin is entirely rolled up into a 10-inch (25-cm) cylinder. Repeat with the remaining stack of bean curd skin and filling. The rolled fish and bean curd skin can be kept in the refrigerator, covered, for about 4 to 5 hours.

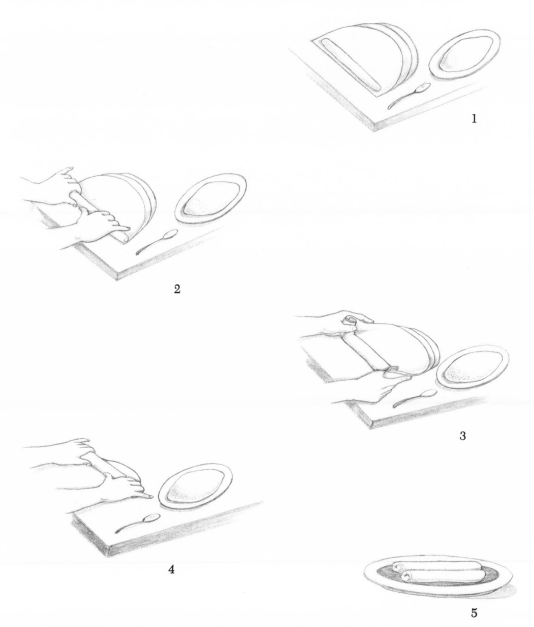

1

2

3

4

5

TO COOK:

5. Using a sharp cleaver, chop each roll diagonally into 1½-inch-long (4-cm) sections. Heat the oil hot. Fry a few pieces of roll at a time for 3 to 4 minutes until golden and crispy. Drain well. Serve hot, with roasted salt and Szechuan peppercorns. (See the recipe for Deep-Fried Shrimp Balls on page 43 for instructions for peppercorn-salt dip.)

NOTE: Shredded presoaked dried mushrooms, bamboo shoots, and bean sprouts, stir-fried with light soy sauce and sugar, can also be wrapped in the dried bean sheets and deep-fried to become a vegetable dish.

Paper-Wrapped Chicken 紙包鷄

Chicken, wrapped in paper and deep-fried, retains its juice and flavor. It is also a fun finger-food to serve. Furthermore, after being deep-fried, the beautiful design —black mushrooms, green parsley leaf, and red ham on the white chicken slice— shows through the paper. It is pretty to look at and delicious to serve as an hors d'oeuvre. Just be sure to remind your guests that the paper should be unwrapped and discarded before eating.

INGREDIENTS:

1 large whole chicken cutlet, or a skinned and boned chicken breast, uncooked
1 Tbs light soy sauce ⎤
1 Tbs Chinese rice wine ⎥
½ tsp salt ⎬ to marinate chicken
½ tsp sugar ⎥
¼ tsp white or black pepper ⎦
5 dried Chinese mushrooms
½ lb (250 g) Smithfield ham
2 Tbs sesame oil
20 squares dry wax paper, 6 by 6 inches (15 by 15 cm)
20 Chinese parsley leaves
2 cups peanut or vegetable oil

PROCEDURES:

1. Cut the chicken cutlet into 1-inch-wide (2.5-cm), 2-inches-long (5-cm), and ¼-inch-thick (6-mm) slices. Marinate with the soy sauce, wine, salt, sugar, and pepper for at least 20 minutes.

2. Soak the mushrooms in hot water for about 15 minutes. Cut off and discard stems. Cut each mushroom into quarters.

3. Trim the fat and skin from the Smithfield ham and boil for about 10 minutes. When cool, cut into small triangular shapes the same size as the mushrooms.

4. Brush some sesame oil on 1 sheet of paper. Place 1 parsley leaf in the middle, and next to it on one side place a mushroom, and on the other side place a ham slice. Then lay a slice of chicken meat on top of all three. Fold like an envelope into a rectangular package. Tuck the corner inside to make a neat package.

TO COOK:

5. Deep-fry the package, a few at a time and face down, at low heat for 2 minutes. Turn them over and fry 30 seconds more. Drain and serve hot. Serve either as an hors d'oeuvre or as one of the main dishes.

NOTE: The paper-wrapped chicken can be deep-fried ahead of time. It can be warmed up in a preheated oven (350° F or 177° C) for about 15 minutes.

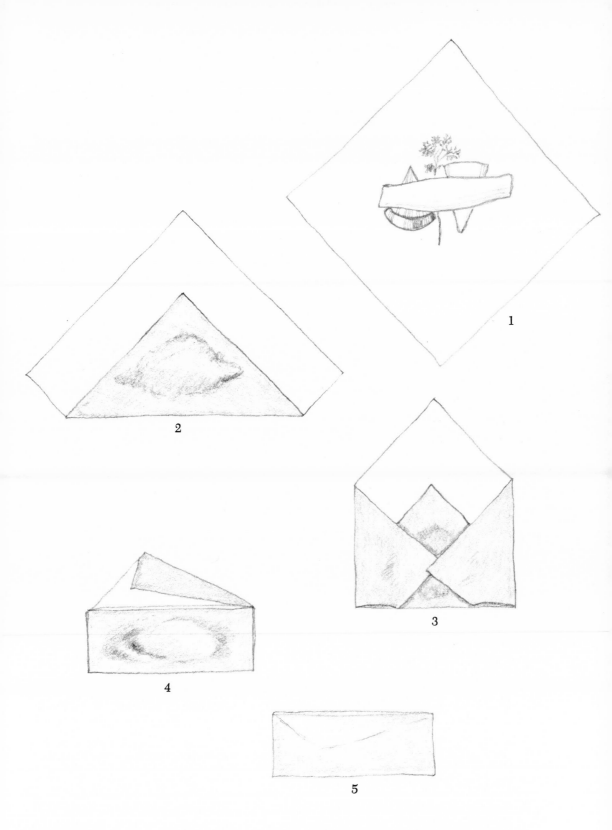

1

2

3

4

5

Squirrel Fish 松鼠魚

This boneless sweet and sour fish, its reddish sauce embellished with onion, carrots, peas, mushrooms, and diced water chestnuts, makes an elegant presentation. The cooked fish is curled back and the tail curved upward and looks somewhat like a baby squirrel, hence the name "squirrel fish." The Chinese usually prefer to cook the fish whole, and banquets generally conclude with the serving of a whole fish, which symbolizes "abundance."

INGREDIENTS:

1½ lbs (750 g) whole fish (sea bass, yellow croaker, striped bass, or yellow pike)

½ tsp salt ⎫
1 Tbs Chinese rice wine ⎬ *to marinate fish*

6 Chinese dried mushrooms

1 carrot
1 small onion
2 cloves garlic
6 fresh water chestnuts
¼ cup frozen peas

2 eggs ⎫
5 Tbs flour ⎪
3 Tbs tapioca starch ⎬ *batter*
5 Tbs water ⎭

1 Tbs dark soy sauce ⎫
1 Tbs Chinese rice wine ⎪
1 tsp salt ⎪
4 Tbs sugar ⎪
4 Tbs white rice vinegar ⎬ *combined seasoning sauce*
4 Tbs catsup ⎪
½ cup chicken broth ⎪
1 tsp sesame oil ⎪
3 tsp tapioca starch ⎭
2 cups peanut or vegetable oil

PROCEDURES:

1. Wash and dry the fish. Cut the head off and set aside. Lay the fish on its side, and with a cleaver split it in half, cutting along the backbone and leaving the pieces joined at the tail; remove and cut off the backbone at the base of the tail. Score the flesh side of fillets with crisscrossing diagonal cuts ½ inch (1.5 cm) apart and almost down to the skin (do not cut through the skin). The fish should be separated into two fillets with the skin intact and joined at the tail. Marinate the fish with salt and wine for at least 10 minutes.

2. Soften the dried mushrooms in hot water. Remove the stems and cut the mushrooms into cubes. Peel and dice the carrot. Dice the onion. Thinly slice the garlic. Peel and dice the water chestnuts. Thaw the peas.

3. Combine the eggs, flour, tapioca starch, and water to make the batter. Mix the ingredients to make the combined seasoning sauce.

TO COOK:

4. Heat the oil in a wok. Dip the fish head in the batter and fry until golden brown. Remove and set aside. Dip the two pieces of fish in the batter and fry the fish about 5 to 6 minutes until firm and brown. Remove. Heat the oil again. Turn the fish to the other side and fry for another minute. Arrange the fried fish on a large platter with the fried head at top. Keep warm in the oven.

5. Remove all but 2 Tbs oil from wok. Stir-fry the garlic slices first, and then the onion and carrots, stirring for 1 minute. Add the mushrooms, peas, and water chestnuts and cook for about 1 minute. Stir in the combined seasoning sauce until thickened and cooked through. Pour it over the fish and serve.

NOTE: The fish head and fish can be deep-fried ahead of time until firm and cooked. Then 15 minutes before serving, heat the oil very hot, deep-fry the fish and head again for about one minute to reheat and to make it golden brown. Remove, keep warm in oven, then cook the sauce and pour it over the fish and serve.

PART II

Dishes Typical of Northern China (Peking, Shantung)

Bok Choy with Bamboo Shoots and Mushrooms

The Chinese are especially fond of green-leaf vegetables like bok choy, which is not only tasty but also provides roughage to the diet. This simple northern dish has become so popular that Chinese from all regions cook it. The Chinese name for it is Three Kinds of Delicacies, and it truly merits its name. The vegetables are briefly stir-fried in hot oil followed by vigorous steam-cooking with a small amount of liquid. This results in a crisp vegetable with vivid coloring that is really extraordinary. After you have learned to cook vegetables this way, you will never want to boil them again.

INGREDIENTS:
1 lb (500 g) bok choy
½ cup bamboo shoots, winter
6 to 8 Chinese dried mushrooms
2 Tbs peanut or vegetable oil
1 tsp salt
½ cup chicken broth
1 Tbs tapioca starch dissolved in 3 Tbs chicken broth

PROCEDURES:
1. Wash the bok choy and cut the stalks and leaves into 1-inch (2.5-cm) pieces. Cut the bamboo shoots into slices ¼ inch (6 mm) thick.

2. Soak the mushrooms in hot water for 15 to 20 minutes. Cut off and discard the stems. Cut the mushrooms in half.

TO COOK:
3. Heat 2 Tbs oil in a wok over high heat. Add 1 tsp salt. Stir-fry the bok choy for about one minute. Add the mushrooms and bamboo shoot slices. Mix well.

4. Add ½ cup chicken broth and bring to a boil. Cover, turn to medium heat, and cook 4 to 5 minutes. Remove cover and mix a few times. Stir the tapioca starch mixture well; add to the wok. Stir well to thicken the sauce. Serve hot.

NOTE: Do not remove the cover out of curiosity or impatience before the vegetables are simmered the full 4 to 5 minutes. The vegetables will turn yellow if the cover is removed and then put on again to cook.

Bok Choy with Abalone Mushrooms 鮑菇炒白菜

This is another way to cook bok choy, and the result is a refreshing, crispy green vegetable embellished with delicate white mushrooms. Abalone mushrooms are a new variety of mushrooms grown in the deep crevasses of high mountains. Their color, flavor, and shape are like abalone, hence their name. This light, mild dish goes very well with a rich or spicy main dish.

INGREDIENTS:
2 lbs (1 kg) bok choy
one 9-oz (250-g) can abalone mushrooms (also called oyster mushrooms)
4 Tbs peanut or vegetable oil
1½ tsp salt
½ tsp sugar
½ cup chicken broth
1 Tbs tapioca starch dissolved in 2 Tbs water

PROCEDURES:

1. Wash the bok choy and cut the stalks and leaves into 2-inch (5-cm) sections.

2. Cut the large abalone mushrooms into smaller pieces. Save the liquid for later use.

TO COOK:

3. Heat the oil in the wok. Add the bok choy gradually and stir-fry until it is thoroughly coated with oil. Add the mushrooms, salt, sugar, the liquid from the mushroom can, and ½ cup chicken broth. Cover and simmer for about 4 to 5 minutes.

4. Give the tapioca starch mixture a quick stir before pouring it into the wok. Stir-fry a few seconds until the sauce thickens. Serve hot.

NOTE: The finished dish can be kept warm in the oven for about 15 to 20 minutes. But do not cover the dish with aluminum foil; otherwise the vegetable will turn yellow.

Chicken with Nuts in Hoisin Sauce 醬爆鷄丁

Chicken is the most honored poultry in China. To show respect to her guests, the Chinese hostess often says, "I have killed a chicken to honor you." Old people and mothers-in-law are very much respected in China; therefore, a chicken dish is often served when they come to visit.

This is a rather simple last-minute dish. Richly coated with the pungent hoisin sauce, the soft-textured diced chicken and mushrooms contrast sharply with the crunchy water chestnuts and bamboo shoots. This has been a favorite dish with practically everyone who has tried the recipe.

INGREDIENTS:

1 whole chicken breast or chicken cutlet, uncooked
½ tsp salt
1 Tbs Chinese rice wine ⎫ *to marinate diced chicken*
1 tsp tapioca starch ⎭
6 to 8 water chestnuts
½ cup bamboo shoots
4 to 6 Chinese dried mushrooms
½ cup peanuts or cashews, raw
6 Tbs peanut or vegetable oil
2 Tbs hoisin sauce

PROCEDURES:

1. Remove bones and skin from the chicken. Cut the meat into ½-inch (1.5-cm) cubes about ¼ inch (6 mm) thick. Marinate with salt, rice wine, and tapioca starch.

2. Dice the water chestnuts; dice the bamboo shoots.

3. Soak the mushrooms in hot water for about 15 to 20 minutes. Remove and discard the stems. Cut them the same size as the water chestnuts.

4. Stir-fry the raw nuts in 4 Tbs oil to lightly brown them. Cool on paper towels.

TO COOK:

5. Heat 2 Tbs oil in a wok over high flame. Add the chicken and stir for about 2 minutes or until the chicken turns white. Add the mushrooms, bamboo shoots, and water chestnuts and stir for another minute.

6. Add 2 Tbs hoisin sauce and mix well. Turn off the heat, add the nuts to the mixture and stir a few times. Serve hot.

NOTE: For readying this dish ahead of time, the preparation should end at step 4. The nuts, when cool, can be stored in a glass jar until ready to use. The final stir-frying is quite simple and takes little time.

Chicken Slices with Straw Mushrooms and Snow Peas 草菇鷄片

As mentioned before, chicken is an esteemed dish in China. Therefore, a chicken dish is often served to special guests to show respect and love.

In this dish the natural color of the chicken is retained, and it contrasts beautifully with the brown umbrella-shaped straw mushrooms and crunchy green snow peas. Though mild in taste, its delicate and refreshing flavor is relished by many.

INGREDIENTS:

1 skinned and boned whole chicken breast or chicken cutlet, uncooked
½ tsp salt
1 Tbs Chinese rice wine ⎫ *to marinate chicken*
1 tsp tapioca starch ⎭
¼ lb (125 g) fresh snow peas
1 tsp tapioca starch
one 8-oz (250-g) can straw mushrooms
2 slices ginger root
3 Tbs peanut or vegetable oil
¼ tsp salt

PROCEDURES:

1. Cut the chicken into slices about 2 inches (5 cm) long and 1 inch (2.5 cm) wide. Marinate with salt, wine, and tapioca starch for at least 30 minutes.

2. Nip off ends and strings of snow peas; parboil.

3. Mix 1 tsp tapioca starch with 2 Tbs liquid from the canned mushrooms. Slice the ginger root into thin slices. Set aside.

TO COOK:

4. Heat 1 Tbs oil in wok. Add ¼ tsp salt and the snow peas. Mix a few times; then add the drained straw mushrooms. Stir and mix for about ½ minute. Remove and set aside.

5. Heat 2 Tbs oil in wok. Drop in ginger slices, then the chicken slices. Stir-fry until all the chicken turns white. Add the snow peas and straw mushrooms. Mix well; stir the tapioca starch mixture, then add to wok. Mix well and serve hot.

NOTE: This is a last-minute stir-fried dish, but the preparations (through step 3) should be done ahead, and the final cooking is quite easy.

Snow Peas with Bamboo Shoots and Mushrooms

This beautiful vegetable dish, one of the first recipes taught in our beginner class, is enjoyed by beginners and advanced students alike. With the stir-fry technique of Chinese cuisine, the cooking time is short, and the vivid colors and the crunchy texture of the vegetables are retained. Simple, pretty, and delicious, it is a dish for all seasons.

INGREDIENTS:
6 to 8 dried Chinese mushrooms
½ lb (250 g) fresh snow peas
3 Tbs peanut or vegetable oil
½ cup winter bamboo shoots, sliced
½ tsp salt
1 Tbs light soy sauce
1 tsp sugar

PROCEDURES:
1. Soak mushrooms in hot water for about 20 minutes. Cut off and discard stems. Cut each into 2 to 4 sections.

2. Trim the ends and strings from the snow peas. Rinse them with cold water, then parboil.

TO COOK:
3. Heat 2 Tbs oil in wok. Add salt first, then the snow peas, stirring constantly for about ½ minute. Remove and set aside.

4. Heat another 1 Tbs oil in wok. Stir in bamboo shoot slices and mushrooms, then add soy sauce and sugar. Stir and cook for 1 minute. Mix in the cooked snow peas and serve immediately.

NOTE: Fresh water chestnuts, sliced, are another ingredient that blends wonderfully well with the rest and also adds another color to this already pretty dish.

Dried Shrimps and Bean Threads Soup 蝦米粉絲湯

Dried shrimps, rather than potato chips, popcorn, or cookies, are the snack that many Chinese like to nibble on when they read or are enjoying a leisurely moment. They are a bit salty and rather flavorful, and can be chewed like gum for a long time. The flavor lingers even after you finish eating them.

Dried shrimps are highly valued by the Chinese as a seasoning, particularly in vegetable dishes and soups. These small shrimps are salted and dried so that their flavor intensifies during the process. Generally they should be soaked in hot water or rice wine for at least 30 minutes before being mixed or cooked with other ingredients. Some Americans are not used to the "fishy" flavor of the dried shrimp. A good way to neutralize the odor is to soak them in Chinese rice wine for at least 30 minutes.

This is a delicate thin soup with a uniquely refreshing taste.

INGREDIENTS:
15 to 20 dried shrimps
2 Tbs Chinese rice wine
2 oz (60 g) bean threads (cellophane noodles)
1 Tbs peanut or vegetable oil
2 stalks scallion, chopped
2 cups chicken broth
½ tsp salt
1 cup water
2 tsp sesame oil

PROCEDURES:
1. Soak the dried shrimps in rice wine for at least 30 minutes. Remove shrimp to a small plate and reserve the wine.

2. Soak the bean threads in hot water for about 10 minutes. Drain and cut into 4-inch-long (10-cm) pieces.

TO COOK:
3. Heat the oil in the wok, add the drained shrimps and chopped scallion and stir-fry for about 1 minute. Splash in the reserved wine. Then add the chicken broth, salt, and water and bring to a boil. Reduce the heat, cover and simmer for 5 minutes.

4. Add the bean threads to the boiling broth. Immediately turn off the heat, garnish with sesame oil, and serve hot.

NOTE: Once the bean threads (cellophane noodles) have been added to the broth, the soup should be served right away or the noodles will absorb all the liquid. Therefore, the soup can be cooked ahead of time only through step 3.

Mu Shu Pork with Pancakes 木樨肉

The Pekinese are especially fond of this typical northern dish. Traditionally it is served with Mandarin pancakes into which one rolls the meat, but it is just as good when served with rice. In Chinese *mu shu* means yellow cassia blossoms. It is called Mu Shu Pork (Cassia Pork) because the eggs added are firmly scrambled and broken into bits resembling the yellow cassia flower.

The tiger lily buds used are called "golden needles" by the Chinese because they are pointed and orange in color. Tree ears are in the mushroom family and are also referred to as "cloud ears" or "wood ears." They are a favorite ingredient in Chinese cooking and add color and crunchiness.

This fluffy, crunchy dish is very popular with both adults and children.

INGREDIENTS:

½ lb (250 g) lean pork (boneless pork loin or pork chop)
1 Tbs Chinese rice wine
2 Tbs black soy sauce
½ tsp sugar   } to marinate pork
1 tsp tapioca starch
4 to 6 dried Chinese mushrooms
2 Tbs dried tree ears (black fungus)
½ cup dried golden needles (tiger lily buds)
1 cup fresh bean sprouts
4 eggs
2 stalks scallions
4 Tbs peanut or vegetable oil
4 Tbs chicken broth
1 tsp sesame oil
1 package frozen Mu Shu pancakes

PROCEDURES:

1. Slice and then shred the pork into thin, 2-inch-long (5-cm) strips. Marinate the shredded pork with the wine, soy sauce, sugar, and tapioca starch.

2. Soak the Chinese mushrooms, tree ears, and golden needles in hot water in separate bowls for 20 minutes. Cut off and discard the stems and shred the mushrooms. Break or cut the tree ears into smaller pieces. Cut the golden needles in half.

3. Rinse and drain the bean sprouts. Beat the eggs and set aside. Shred the scallions into 2-inch-long sections.

TO COOK:

4. Scramble the eggs in 2 Tbs oil into dry fine pieces. Set aside.

5. Heat 2 Tbs oil in the wok; stir-fry the marinated pork for about 2 minutes. Add mushrooms, tree ears, golden needles, and scallions and mix well. Add 4 Tbs of chicken broth and bring to boil.

6. Add the scrambled eggs and bean sprouts and mix thoroughly. Garnish with sesame oil. Serve with pancakes.

NOTE: To serve with pancakes: Defrost the frozen pancakes. Open the package and separate into 10 thin pancakes. Fold the pancakes twice like a napkin and arrange them in a circle on a steamer rack, overlapping just a little. Steam about 1 minute. Since the pancakes are very thin, oversteaming will make them soggy and stick together. Open each pancake; put a little Mu Shu Pork filling in the middle, wrap it up like an egg roll and eat.

Peking Hot and Sour Soup 北京酸辣湯

This is a hearty soup, ideal for winter meals. It originated in Peking where the winter months are long and cold.

In China, soup is eaten throughout the meal as the principal beverage. Tea is only served before and immediately after each meal to help digestion.

The Chinese never drink cold water during a meal. They believe that the oil used in cooking and cold water do not mix well for one's health. Therefore, a bowl of soup is often served to accompany the food. If the meal is long, hot soup is often brought to the table in the middle of the meal to replenish the supply.

INGREDIENTS:
4 oz (120 g) lean pork
1 tsp Chinese rice wine } *to marinate pork*
½ tsp tapioca starch
4 Chinese dried mushrooms
2 Tbs dried tree ears
¼ cup dried lily flowers
¼ cup bamboo shoots
1 Tbs Szechuan preserved vegetable (Jar Choy)
1 cake fresh bean curd
4 cups chicken broth
½ tsp salt
½ tsp sugar
1 tsp light soy sauce
2 Tbs Chin Kiang vinegar
¼ tsp white or black pepper
2 Tbs tapioca starch dissolved in 3 Tbs water
1 egg, beaten
1 tsp sesame oil
1 stalk scallion, chopped

PROCEDURES:
1. Shred the pork into thin, 2-inch-long (5-cm) strips. Mix the shredded pork with the wine and tapioca starch.

2. Soak the Chinese mushrooms, tree ears, and lily flowers in hot water in separate bowls for about 15 to 20 minutes. Cut off and discard the stems from mushrooms and shred them; break or cut the large pieces of tree ears into smaller pieces; and cut the lily flowers in halves. Shred the bamboo shoots.

3. Slice and then shred the Szechuan preserved vegetable. Shred the bean curd into long lean strips.

TO COOK:
4. Put chicken broth, salt, sugar, soy sauce, and the shredded Szechuan preserved vegetable in a saucepan and bring to a boil. Stir in the pork mixture. After boiling for 1 minute, add the shredded mushrooms, tree ears, lily flowers, and

shredded bamboo shoots. Boil for another minute. Add the shredded bean curd, vinegar, and pepper.

5. Bring the soup to a boil again. Stir in the well-mixed tapioca starch until it thickens. Mix in beaten egg and remove from heat immediately.

6. Garnish with sesame oil and scallion. Serve hot.

NOTE: This soup can and should be done ahead of time, because the longer it sits, the stronger and tastier it becomes. Just be sure that you stop at the end of step 4, and leave it in the pot on the stove. Once the soup has been thickened and the beaten egg has been added, it should be served right away.

Shrimp Toasts 蝦仁吐司

Crunchy and tasty, shrimp toasts are excellent finger foods to be served as hors d'oeuvres. In China, they are usually served as snacks or as one of the main dishes in a buffet dinner. Since the Chinese are not, by and large, a drinking nation, they do not have a cocktail time before dinner for serving hors d'oeuvres. Wine is served only on special occasions, for example, New Year's and wedding banquets. At banquets, the Chinese drink and play "finger games" similar to those played by the Italians. The difference is that in China the loser of the game, rather than the winner, drinks.

INGREDIENTS:
½ lb (250 g) frozen, peeled and deveined shrimps
6 fresh water chestnuts
2 Tbs ground pork fat or fatty bacon
1 egg, lightly beaten
1 Tbs Chinese rice wine
1 tsp salt
½ tsp sugar
1 Tbs tapioca starch
one ½-inch (1.5-cm) piece fresh ginger root
6 slices white bread, at least 2 days old
24 leaves fresh Chinese parsley
2 cups peanut or vegetable oil

PROCEDURES:
1. Defrost and rinse the shrimps. Pat dry thoroughly. With a food processor or a cleaver, chop the shrimp to a fine, pulplike mass.

2. Peel the fresh water chestnuts and chop them fine. Mix the minced shrimp, chopped water chestnuts, and ground pork fat with the lightly beaten egg, wine, salt, sugar, and tapioca starch. Squeeze the ginger with a garlic press and add the juice to the mixture. Mix thoroughly to form a paste. Set aside.

3. Trim the crust off each slice of bread. Cut each slice into 4 triangles. Spread about 1 tsp shrimp mixture over each triangle and then place one parsley leaf on top.

TO COOK:
4. Heat the oil in a wok to 375° F or 182° C. Gently lower the bread into the oil with the shrimp side down. After 1 minute, turn over and fry for a few more seconds. Fry only a few at a time. When golden brown, drain on paper towels. Serve immediately.

NOTE: The fried shrimp toasts can be frozen and then reheated in a preheated oven (375° F or 182° C) for about 15 minutes.

Shredded Chicken with Bean Sprouts 銀芽雞絲

This is a very presentable dish. The white velvety chicken, shredded long and lean, combines beautifully with the shredded reddish ham, crunchy green snow peas, and crispy white bean sprouts. In addition, the softer texture of the chicken and ham contrasts nicely with the crunchy snow peas and bean sprouts. It is a dish definitely worth trying.

INGREDIENTS:

1 whole skinned and boned chicken breast or chicken cutlet, uncooked
½ egg white
½ tsp salt ⎫
2 tsp tapioca starch ⎬ to marinate chicken
1 Tbs Chinese rice wine ⎭
2 cups fresh bean sprouts
¼ cup Smithfield ham, cooked and shredded to 2-inch (5-cm) strips
5 Tbs peanut or vegetable oil
2 stalks scallions, cut into 2-inch (5-cm) lengths
¼ lb (125 g) fresh snow peas, shredded to 2-inch (5-cm) strips
1 tsp salt
½ tsp sugar
1 Tbs tapioca starch dissolved in 2 Tbs water

PROCEDURES:

1. Shred the chicken into 2-inch-long (5-cm) strips. Marinate with egg white, salt, tapioca starch, and wine for 20 to 30 minutes.

2. Soak the bean sprouts in cold water. Drain well before cooking. Boil the Smithfield ham for about 10 minutes; when cool, cut the ham into 2-inch-long (5-cm) strips. Shred the fresh snow peas into the same length as other ingredients.

TO COOK:

3. Heat the wok very hot. Add 5 Tbs oil; first drop in the scallion and then the chicken, stirring quickly for about 1 minute. Remove the chicken with a strainer and set aside. Leave the remaining oil in the wok.

4. Heat the remaining oil in the wok. Add bean sprouts and snow peas and stir-fry for 1 minute; then add salt and sugar. Stir and mix well. Finally add the ham and cooked chicken; mix well. Mix the tapioca starch and water very well and add to the chicken, stirring over high heat until the liquid thickens and coats the chicken with a clear glaze. Serve hot.

NOTE: If there are more than two last-minute stir-frying dishes for you to prepare, this dish can be done ahead of time up to step 3.

Shredded Pork in Peking Sauce 京醬肉絲

This succulent Northern-style dish is served on a bed of shredded scallions. Although this famous dish is often served on the banquet table, it is quite simple to prepare and takes little time to cook.

INGREDIENTS:

1 lb (500 g) boneless lean pork or 4 pork chops
1½ Tbs dark soy sauce
1 Tbs Chinese rice wine   } to marinate pork
1 Tbs tapioca starch
8 stalks scallions
3 Tbs sweet bean sauce
2 tsp sugar
1 Tbs Chinese rice wine
4 Tbs peanut or vegetable oil

PROCEDURES:

1. Shred pork into long, thin strips about 2 inches (5 cm) long. Marinate with the soy sauce, wine, and tapioca starch for at least 20 minutes.

2. Cut the scallions diagonally into 2-inch-long (5-cm) thin pieces. Put on a plate.

3. Combine the bean sauce with the sugar and 1 Tbs wine.

TO COOK:

4. Heat 3 Tbs oil in a wok. Stir-fry the shredded pork for about 1 minute until done. Remove and put aside. Drain oil from wok.

5. Heat 1 Tbs oil. Stir-fry the sweet bean paste mixture for about 10 seconds. Add pork; stir thoroughly. Remove and place on the scallions. Before eating, mix the pork and scallions well.

NOTE: In order that the final product have the desired look, the scallions should be shredded diagonally into long lean strips and the pork also shredded long and thin. Beef steak can be used as a substitute for pork.

Chinese Cabbage Salad with Hot Chili Oil 辣白菜

Simple and spicy, this cold cabbage dish is often included in the Assorted Cold Platter, usually the first course of a banquet. It can also be served separately as a side dish or vegetable dish. Crisp and crunchy, this sweet and sour cabbage dish from Peking is remarkably refreshing.

INGREDIENTS:

1½ lbs (750 g) Chinese cabbage (white parts only)
2 tsp salt
1 tsp fresh ginger, grated
1 Tbs peanut or vegetable oil
5 Tbs sugar
¼ cup white rice vinegar
1 tsp hot chili oil (or more or less to taste)

PROCEDURES:

1. Wash the cabbage with cold water. Cut the cabbage stalks into 2-inch (5-cm) sections; then shred them into ¼- by 2-inch (6-mm by 5-cm) strips. (You should have about 6 cups.) Place the shredded cabbage stalks in a container and sprinkle the salt over them. Mix well, pack down, and let stand for about 1 hour.

2. Squeeze out liquid from the cabbage. Add grated ginger, mix well, and pack down again.

TO COOK:

3. In a saucepan or wok, bring the oil, sugar, and vinegar to a boil. Pour the liquid over the cabbage, cover and let stand for ½ hour. Then pour the liquid back into the saucepan. Bring it to a boil and pour it over the cabbage a second time. Cover and chill.

4. Take out the cabbage and pour off the excess juice. Add hot chili oil to the cabbage. Mix well and place on a plate. Serve cold.

NOTE: After completing step 3, the cabbage and liquid can be covered and kept in the refrigerator for several weeks. Shredded carrots (about ½ cup) can be added and marinated with the cabbage for color.

Fillet of Fish with Wine Rice Sauce 糟溜魚片

This elegant dish originated in Shantung Province. Wine rice is used to give it a rich wine flavor and a thick consistency. Wine rice is fermented rice made from glutinous rice, using wine yeast as the fermenting agent. It takes 2 to 3 days for the fermentation to take place, and once made, wine rice can be stored in a glass jar and left in the refrigerator for weeks. Wine rice can be purchased in Chinese grocery stores.

The sauce from this dish is glazed and tasty. The crunchy black tree ears also contrast beautifully with the tender white fish slices.

INGREDIENTS:

1 lb (500 g) fillet of flounder, gray sole, yellow pike, or sea bass
1 Tbs Chinese rice wine ⎫
1 tsp salt ⎪
½ egg white ⎬ to marinate fish fillet
1 Tbs tapioca starch ⎭
¼ cup tree ears
2 cloves garlic
½ cup fermented wine rice ⎫
2 Tbs Chinese rice wine ⎪
½ tsp salt ⎬ combined sauce
½ tsp sugar ⎪
2 tsp tapioca starch ⎭
6 Tbs peanut or vegetable oil

PROCEDURES:

1. Remove any bones from the center of the fillet. Cut the fillet lengthwise into two strips; slice each half almost parallel to the grain but at a slight angle into 2- by 2-inch (5- by 5-cm) squares. Marinate with wine, salt, egg white, and tapioca starch for at least 15 to 20 minutes.

2. Soak the tree ears in boiling hot water for 30 minutes. Drain and set aside. Thinly slice the garlic. Set aside with the tree ears.

3. Use a double layer of cheesecloth to squeeze out the wine rice juice; add water and squeeze again to make ½ cup wine rice juice. Discard the rice. Add wine, salt, sugar, and tapioca starch as listed above in the combined sauce.

TO COOK:

4. Heat a wok very hot, add oil and heat to about 300° F (150° C). (Beginners may want to use a thermostat.) Add the fish and gently stir until most of the color has changed. With a strainer, remove the fish to a plate.

5. Heat the remaining oil and stir-fry the garlic and tree ears. Stir the combined sauce well, add to the wok, mix a few times. Add the cooked fish; stir gently and cook just to heat through. Serve immediately.

NOTE: Since the cooking time is rather short, this dish will taste best when done as a last-minute stir-fried dish. Stir the fish slices gently to avoid breaking them.

Stir-Fried Diced Chicken in Bird's Nest 雀巢鷄 [

This extraordinarily pretty dish is fun to serve. The succulent but firm chicken cubes, embellished with colorful water chestnuts, carrots, green pepper, and straw mushrooms, are served in an edible bird's nest made with potato sticks. This elegant dish proves that the Chinese consider every possible way to make food appeal to the senses. It is definitely a banquet dish, excellent for entertaining; upon its presentation you are sure to receive a torrent of compliments.

INGREDIENTS:

2 whole chicken cutlets or chicken breast, skinned and boned
1 Tbs light soy sauce ⎫
1 Tbs Chinese rice wine ⎬ *to marinate chicken*
1 egg white ⎪
1½ Tbs tapioca starch ⎭
½ cup carrots, sliced
½ can (7½ oz or 225 g) straw mushrooms
1 cup green pepper, diced to ½-inch (1½-cm) pieces
½ cup fresh water chestnuts, peeled and sliced
2 stalks scallions, chopped
1 Tbs ginger, chopped
2 Tbs light soy sauce ⎫
1 Tbs Chinese rice wine ⎪
¼ tsp salt ⎪
½ tsp sugar ⎬ *combined seasoning sauce*
¼ tsp white or black pepper ⎪
1 tsp sesame oil ⎪
½ Tbs tapioca starch ⎭
1 lb (500 g) potatoes
½ tsp salt
1 cup tapioca starch
6 cups peanut or vegetable oil for deep-frying
some broccoli flowerets ⎫
some straw mushrooms ⎬ *for decoration*
7 Tbs peanut or vegetable oil for stir-frying

PROCEDURES:

1. Dice the chicken into ½-inch pieces. Marinate with the marinade ingredients listed above for 20 to 30 minutes.

2. Parboil the carrot slices in boiling water for about 1 minute. Drain the straw mushrooms. Assemble the carrots, mushrooms, diced pepper, sliced water chestnuts, scallion and ginger.

3. Mix the combined sauce ingredients.

4. Peel and shred the potatoes into long, thin strips. Rinse under cold water; drain and dry. Mix with ½ tsp salt and 1 cup tapioca starch. Put the potato shreds in one strainer and press upon it lightly another strainer and submerge both in 6

cups of very hot oil. Deep-fry for about 4 minutes until golden brown. Turn the strainer upside down and tap on the strainer until the bird's nest comes loose. Place the bird's nest on a serving plate.

5. Break off the flowerets from the broccoli. Parboil the flowerets in boiling water for about 1 minute. Rinse in cold water. Arrange the flowerets and straw mushrooms attractively around the nest on the serving plate.

TO COOK:

6. Heat 4 Tbs oil in wok. Stir-fry the marinated diced chicken until the meat turns white. Drain and remove.

7. Heat 3 Tbs oil in wok. Sauté carrots, mushrooms, green pepper, water chestnuts, scallion, and ginger for a few seconds. Add chicken cubes and combined seasoning sauce. Mix well, pour into the bird's nest, and serve hot.

NOTE: The bird's nest can be made and deep-fried ahead of time and later re-heated in a preheated 300° F (150° C) oven. The traditional way to eat this dish is to first serve the chicken and vegetables in the nest; afterward the delicious nest is broken up and nibbled by the diners.

Fried Whole Fish in Sweet and Sour Sauce 糖醋全鱼

Sweet and sour whole fish is often served as the finale at a Chinese banquet to symbolize "abundance" since *yü*, the Chinese word for fish, has the same sound as the word for "plentiful" or "abundance." In some parts of China, the whole fish is served in the New Year banquet, but never touched or eaten. It is considered a good omen because there will always be food left over in the coming year.

The water chestnut powder is made from ground water chestnuts. It is extremely fine and light and is often used for coating when you want the crust to be exceptionally light. Once open, it should be transferred to a bottle where it will keep indefinitely.

INGREDIENTS:

1½ lb (750 g) whole fish (carp, sea bass, striped bass, or quick-frozen Chinese yellow croaker)

1 stalk scallion, cut into inch lengths ⎫
4 slices ginger root ⎬ to marinate fish
1 tsp salt ⎪
1½ Tbs Chinese rice wine ⎭

6 to 8 Chinese dried mushrooms
3 stalks scallion, shredded
¼ cup ginger root, shredded
6 to 8 fresh water chestnuts

5 Tbs sugar ⎫
5 Tbs Chin Kiang vinegar ⎪
8 Tbs water ⎪
3 Tbs catsup ⎬ combined seasoning sauce
½ Tbs tapioca starch ⎪
1 tsp salt ⎪
1 tsp sesame oil ⎭

¼ cup tapioca starch ⎫ to coat fish
¼ cup water chestnut powder ⎭

3 cups peanut or vegetable oil for deep-frying
2 Tbs peanut or vegetable oil for stir-frying

PROCEDURES:

1. Clean the fish and dry well with paper towels. Make several diagonal cuts almost touching the bone on both sides of the fish. Rub the scallion, ginger, salt, and wine mixture all over the fish, inside the belly and into the slashes. Let the fish stand at room temperature for about 30 minutes.

2. Soak the dried mushrooms in hot water until soft, about 15 minutes. Remove and discard the stems, and shred the mushrooms. Set aside with shredded scallions and ginger.

3. Peel and then chop the fresh water chestnuts. Mix with the ingredients listed above to make the combined seasoning sauce. Set aside for later use.

4. Mix ¼ cup tapioca starch with ¼ cup water chestnut powder. Coat the fish all over with the mixture, inside the belly and slashes as well. Cover and refrigerate until ready to be deep-fried.

TO COOK:

5. Heat the oil in a wok until very hot, about 375° F (182° C). (Beginners may want to use a thermostat.) Gently slide in the fish and deep-fry for 5 to 6 minutes on each side, basting and shifting occasionally, until golden brown and crispy. Place the fried fish on a serving platter so that it sits upright on its belly. With a towel, hold and press down gently on the neck of the fish so that the slashed sides of the belly protrude. Keep warm in oven.

6. Heat another 2 Tbs oil in wok. Stir-fry the shredded scallions, ginger, and mushrooms over high heat, then add the combined seasoning sauce. Stir until it thickens, then pour it over the fried fish. Serve hot.

NOTE: The fish can be deep-fried ahead of time and left at room temperature. Half an hour before serving, deep-fry the fish again in very hot oil for 2 to 3 minutes until golden brown and hot. Then keep it warm in the oven while you prepare the sauce.

Peking Duck   北京烤鸭

Peking Duck first came from Shantung Province, but later became famous by the name "Peking." Shantung is near Peking, where the Imperial Court was located. Therefore, many fine Shantung dishes were adopted by the aristocracy and became their own.

Peking Duck, an important dish, is usually served in the latter part of formal dinners and banquets. The skin, which should be crispy, fluffy, and not greasy, is the most important part of the dish. But the meat should also be juicy and tender.

When served at a simple dinner in Peking, one eats the skin and meat wrapped in Mandarin pancakes, followed by a soup made of Chinese cabbage cooked in the broth made from the leftover duck bones. In a banquet, only the skin and meat are served with pancakes along with scallions and hoisin sauce.

INGREDIENTS:
5 lb (2½ kg) fresh or frozen duck
1½ inch (4 cm) ginger root
1 stalk scallion
3 Tbs honey
6 cups water
2 Tbs Chinese rice wine
1 Tbs white rice vinegar
3 Tbs tapioca starch dissolved in ½ cup water
1 tsp sesame oil ⎫
¼ cup hoisin sauce ⎪
2 tsp sugar ⎬ *sauce*
2 Tbs water ⎭
10 small scallions
20 Mandarin pancakes (frozen)

PROCEDURES:

1. Remove excess fat from the body of the duck. Rinse with water, drain, and dry well. Hang the duck up with a string in a cool, airy place for at least 4 hours (to speed up drying, the duck can be hung in front of an air conditioner or fan for 2 to 3 hours).

2. Crush the ginger with the flat side of a cleaver; cut the scallion in half. Combine the ginger and scallion with 3 Tbs honey and 6 cups of water in a wok. Boil for 2 minutes. Add the rice wine and vinegar, and stir in the tapioca starch and water mixture. Bring to a boil again. Holding the duck by its string, lower it into the boiling liquid. Turn the duck from side to side until every part of the skin has been moistened. Lift the duck and repeat the dipping once more. Remove the duck and hang it in front of an air conditioner or fan for 2 to 3 hours.

3. To make the sauce, combine sesame oil, hoisin sauce, and sugar in a small saucepan. Stir and cook for 1 minute. Add water and cook for about ½ minute. Pour into a sauce dish. Set aside.

4. Use only the white parts of the scallions. Use a sharp knife to make length-wise slits about 1-inch (2.5-cm) long on each end. Place in a bowl of ice water for 10 minutes or until the cut parts curl up like brushes. Place the scallions around the sauce on the sauce dish.

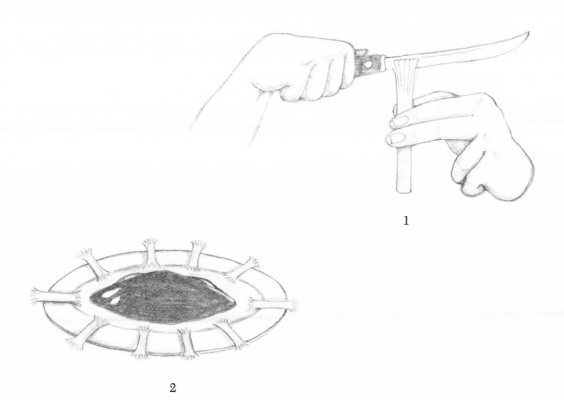

1

2

TO COOK:

5. Put the duck breast side up on a roasting rack. Place the rack in a broiler pan filled with 1 to 2 inches of water. Preheat the oven to 350° F (177° C). Roast the duck for 2 to 3 hours until dark brown.

6. Remove the skin from the meat. Cut the skin and meat of the duck into 2-by 3-inch (5- by 7.5-cm) pieces, respectively, and arrange nicely on a plate. Place one piece each of skin and meat in a pancake. Dip the scallion into the sauce and put it in the pancake also. Roll up the pancake into a cylinder and eat with fingers.

NOTE: Since the preparation is far more involved than the cooking, it should be done one day ahead. About 3 hours before serving, just place the duck in the oven and roast until dark brown. The frozen Mandarin pancakes usually come 10 in a package. Defrost and then separate them into 10 sheets. Fold each twice like a napkin and arrange in a circle on a steamer rack and steam about 1 minute; serve immediately.

PART III

Dishes Typical of Western China (Szechuan and Hunan)

Ants on the Trees 螞蟻上樹

Though at first glance the name of this dish can be shocking to those who have never had it, Ants on the Trees is really a delicious, spicy dish made with ground pork, which represents the ants, dotted over cellophane noodles, which symbolize tree branches. The hot bean sauce lifts this dish from the ordinary with its mildly spicy taste.

Instead of soaking the cellophane noodles, they can be deep-fried, a few at a time, in very hot oil (about 400° F or 204° C) for a few seconds on each side until puffed up. Place the fried noodles on a serving plate. Marinate the ground pork as listed below. Stir-fry the meat with the scallions until separated and cooked. Add the hot bean sauce and sugar, stir and mix well. Pour over the noodles and serve.

INGREDIENTS:
2 oz (60 g) cellophane noodles
½ lb (250 g) ground pork
1 Tbs dark soy sauce
1 Tbs Chinese rice wine } *to marinate ground pork*
1 tsp tapioca starch
3 Tbs peanut or vegetable oil for stir-frying
2 stalks scallions, chopped
4 tsp hot bean sauce
1 tsp sugar
1 cup chicken broth

PROCEDURES:

1. Soak cellophane noodles in warm water for 20 minutes. Drain and cut into 4-inch-long (10-cm) sections.

2. Marinate the ground pork with soy sauce, wine, and tapioca starch as listed above.

TO COOK:

3. Heat 3 Tbs oil in wok; add the scallion and then the ground pork. Stir-fry until the meat separates. Add the hot bean sauce and sugar; stir and mix well. Add the cellophane noodles, stir and blend with the meat. Pour in chicken broth and bring to a boil. Cover and cook about 5 minutes until the broth is absorbed, stirring twice. Serve hot.

NOTE: The finished dish can be covered with aluminum foil and kept warm in the oven. Ground veal or beef can be used instead of pork, but the flavor will not be as good.

Dry-Cooked String Beans 干扁四季豆

These wrinkled, tender green beans, speckled with tasty ground pork and preserved vegetables, make a lovely presentation. Although no sauce remains after this dish has been cooked, the beans are unusually delicious with the lingering flavor they absorb in cooking.

Preserved vegetables are often used in Chinese cooking to add zest to vegetables and to bring out flavor. The Tientsin preserved winter vegetables used here are what give this dish its unique taste. They are chopped Chinese cabbage preserved with salt, garlic, and spices. They have a deep flavor and are also good with simmered meats or poultry.

INGREDIENTS:
1 lb (500 g) Chinese long beans or string beans
¼ lb (125 g) ground pork
1 tsp light soy sauce
1 tsp Chinese rice wine
½ tsp salt } *to marinate ground pork*
1 tsp sugar
1½ cups peanut or vegetable oil
2 tsp ginger root, finely chopped
4 Tbs preserved winter vegetables (Tientsin preserved cabbage)
4 Tbs chicken broth
1 tsp sesame oil

PROCEDURES:
1. Rinse the long beans and then cut them into 3-inch-long (7.5-cm) pieces.
2. Marinate the ground pork with the soy sauce, wine, salt, and sugar, and set aside.
3. Heat the oil in the wok; deep-fry the green beans until they are wrinkled (about 3 minutes). Remove beans and drain oil from wok.

TO COOK:
4. Put back only 2 Tbs of oil in wok. Add ginger, then ground pork and stir-fry until the pork changes color. Add preserved winter vegetables, stir a few times. Then add chicken broth and green beans. Stir over high heat until the sauce is gone.
5. Garnish with sesame oil. Serve hot or cold.

NOTE: The string beans should be deep-fried ahead of time and can be left at room temperature for several hours. They will have to be stir-fried to warm them up later on. This dish also tastes delicious when served cold. Szechuan preserved kohlrabi can be used instead of Tientsin preserved vegetables.

Sautéed Bean Curd, Family Style 家常豆腐

Bean curd, known to the Orientals as *to fu*, is high in protein, mild in taste, and quite inexpensive. It is considered the life-sustaining food for the vegetarians in the Orient. Americans, especially those conscious of nutrition, are beginning to cook with *to fu*, largely because of its high-protein, low-calorie, low-cholesterol value.

Bean curd is the most versatile and important vegetable product in Chinese cuisine. Bland, absorbent, soft-textured but strong, it combines well with many ingredients and is conducive to all types of cooking. The family-style bean curd is excellent for introducing *to fu* to your family or friends. After being deep-fried, the bean curd becomes firm and spongy instead of soft and smooth. Speckled with ground pork and seasoned with hot bean sauce, garlic, and ginger, this dish is mildly spicy and delicious with a rich brown sauce.

INGREDIENTS:
4 cakes Chinese bean curd
1 cup peanut or vegetable oil
¼ lb (125 g) ground pork
1 Tbs hot bean paste
1 Tbs garlic, minced
1 tsp ginger, chopped
⅔ cup chicken broth
1 tsp sugar
1 tsp salt
1 Tbs tapioca starch dissolved in 2 Tbs water
2 stalks scallions, chopped ⎫
1 tsp sesame oil ⎭ *for garnishing*

PROCEDURES:

1. Cut the bean curd into 1½-inch (4-cm) square pieces. Cut each square diagonally into two triangles. Then cut each piece horizontally to a thickness of about ¼ inch (6 mm).

2. Heat the oil in a wok. Deep-fry the bean curd pieces (put in enough to be covered with the oil) until they are golden brown. Remove the bean curd from the wok and reduce oil to 2 Tbs.

TO COOK:

3. Heat the 2 Tbs oil in wok. Stir-fry the ground pork for 1 minute. Then add the hot bean paste, garlic, and ginger, stirring constantly. Finally add chicken broth, browned bean curd, sugar, and salt. Bring to a boil, then cover the wok and cook over low heat for about 3 minutes.

4. Thicken the sauce with tapioca paste. Garnish with chopped scallion and sesame oil. Serve hot.

NOTE: The triangular bean curd pieces can be, and should be, deep-fried earlier and left at room temperature. They will be reheated in the final stir-frying.

Kung Pao Chicken
(Diced Chicken with Dried Red Peppers) 宮保鷄丁

Tender chicken cubes and crunchy peanuts, served with a glistening, spicy sauce, is a good dish to introduce your friends to Szechuan cooking. Diced pork can be used instead of chicken in this recipe for Kung Pao Pork.

INGREDIENTS:

1 *whole skinned and boned chicken breast or cutlet, uncooked*
1 *Tbs Chinese rice wine* ⎫
1 *Tbs tapioca starch* ⎬ *to marinate diced chicken*
1 *Tbs light soy sauce* ⎭
¼ *lb (125 g) raw peanuts*
7 *Tbs peanut or vegetable oil for stir-frying*
1 *Tbs light soy sauce* ⎫
1 *Tbs Chinese rice wine* ⎪
1 *Tbs sugar* ⎪
1 *tsp tapioca starch* ⎬ *combined seasoning sauce (Kung Pao sauce)*
½ *Tbs Chin Kiang vinegar* ⎪
1 *Tbs sesame oil* ⎭
8 *to 10 dried red peppers*
1 *tsp ginger root, finely chopped*

PROCEDURES:

1. Cut chicken into 1-inch (2.5-cm) cubes and marinate with wine, tapioca starch, and soy sauce as listed above for 20 to 30 minutes.

2. Stir-fry raw peanuts in 4 Tbs of oil over medium heat until golden brown. Remove and cool on paper towel.

3. Combine the ingredients listed above to make the combined seasoning sauce.

TO COOK:

4. Heat 2 Tbs oil in wok. Drop in diced chicken and stir-fry until the color turns white (about 1½ minutes). Remove and set aside.

5. Heat 1 Tbs oil in wok. Stir-fry the dried red peppers until they become black; add the chopped ginger and chicken, stirring constantly. Then add the combined seasoning sauce and mix thoroughly. Turn off heat, then mix in peanuts. Serve hot.

NOTE: Since the final cooking time is but a few minutes, this dish is best when served as a last-minute stir-fried dish.

Sweet and Sour Cabbage, Szechuan Style 辣白菜

This simple vegetable dish is extremely refreshing with its crisp cabbage and the sweet and sour sauce which resembles a hot dressing. It is also excellent when cooked a day ahead of time and served as a cold dish.

INGREDIENTS:

1 lb (500 g) Chinese cabbage
2 Tbs light soy sauce ⎫
½ tsp salt ⎪
2 Tbs sugar ⎬ combined seasoning sauce
2 Tbs white rice vinegar ⎪
½ tsp tapioca starch ⎭
2 Tbs peanut or vegetable oil
6 to 8 dried red peppers (whole)

PROCEDURES:

1. Wash the cabbage and cut into 1- by 1½-inch (2.5- by 4-cm) pieces.
2. Combine soy sauce, salt, sugar, vinegar, and tapioca starch in a bowl. Set aside.

TO COOK:

3. Heat a wok, add oil, and stir-fry the dried red peppers until black. Add cabbage and keep stirring over high heat for 2 minutes.
4. Stir the sauce in the bowl to make sure the sugar has dissolved. Add the sauce to the wok. Stir and mix well over high heat for another minute. Serve hot or cold.

NOTE: If the dried red peppers are omitted, this dish becomes the famous Peking-style sweet and sour cabbage.

Ma Po Bean Curd 麻婆豆腐

As mentioned before, bean curd (*to fu*) is high in protein and low in calories and cholesterol. Since it is so nutritious and represents such a good buy, we Chinese use "eating bean curd" to mean "taking advantage of or flirting with a person."

This tasty Szechuan dish, called "Grandma's Bean Curd" by the Chinese, is mildly spicy with a light-colored glazed sauce. The bean curd is smooth and tender, speckled with the ground pork. The Szechuan peppercorn powder used for garnishing here gives this dish a distinctive final touch.

INGREDIENTS:

¼ lb (125 g) ground pork
1 Tbs dark soy sauce
1 Tbs Chinese rice wine ⎱ to marinate ground pork
½ tsp sugar ⎰
2 tsp Szechuan peppercorn
4 cakes firm Chinese bean curd or 2 cakes soft bean curd
¼ tsp dried red pepper, chopped ⎫
1 tsp ginger root, chopped
2 stalks scallions, chopped
1 Tbs hot bean sauce ⎬ combined seasoning sauce
¼ cup chicken broth
1 tsp salt ⎭
3 Tbs peanut or vegetable oil
1 Tbs tapioca starch dissolved in 2 Tbs chicken broth
2 tsp sesame oil

PROCEDURES:

1. In a bowl, marinate the ground pork with soy sauce, wine, and sugar for 15 to 20 minutes.

2. Stir the Szechuan peppercorn in a wok (without oil) over medium heat for about 2 minutes or until they are lightly browned. Then crush the peppercorn to a fine powder and set aside.

3. Cut the bean curd into small cubes. Set aside. Combine the chopped red pepper, ginger, and scallions with the hot bean sauce, chicken broth, and salt to make the combined sauce. Set aside.

TO COOK:

4. Heat 3 Tbs of oil in the wok; swirl it about in the wok. Drop in the pork mixture and stir-fry for about 2 or 3 minutes until it changes color and separates.

5. Add the bean curd and then the combined sauce, and cook over moderate heat for 2 to 3 minutes.

6. Thicken with the tapioca starch mixture. Then garnish with sesame oil and Szechuan peppercorn powder. Serve hot.

NOTE: This dish can be cooked ahead of time, covered, and kept warm in the oven for about half an hour.

Steamed Fish, Hunan Style 豆豉辣椒蒸魚

This Hunan-style steamed fish is beautiful and delicious. Though spicy hot, the fish meat is tender and juicy, with the rich flavors of fermented black beans, ginger, and scallions. The diced Smithfield ham not only enhances the taste but also adds color to this dish. Simple to prepare and easy to cook (just steam), this is an excellent dish to serve your family and friends.

INGREDIENTS:

1½ lb (750 g) *whole sea bass, striped bass, or sea trout*
1 tsp *salt*
2 Tbs *fermented black beans, coarsely chopped*
1 tsp *dried red pepper, diced*
1 Tbs *Smithfield ham, cooked and chopped*
1 Tbs *light soy sauce*
1 Tbs *Chinese rice wine*   } *combined seasoning sauce*
1 Tbs *ginger root, chopped*
1 stalk *scallion, chopped*
½ tsp *salt*
1 Tbs *peanut or vegetable oil*

PROCEDURES:

1. Clean and wash the fish. Dry inside and out. Slash both sides of the fish diagonally at 1½-inch (4-cm) intervals. Rub a little salt (1 tsp) inside and out and let it marinate for about 10 minutes. Put the whole fish into a shallow, heatproof dish or bowl. (If the fish is too long, cut it in half crosswise to steam. After steaming restore the fish to its original length and cover the opening with the sauce ingredients and some additional shredded scallions.)

2. Combine the black beans, diced red peppers, ham, soy sauce, wine, ginger, scallion, salt, and oil as listed in the combined sauce ingredients. Pour the sauce ingredients all over the fish. Refrigerate until ready to steam.

TO COOK:

3. First boil the water. Place the shallow bowl with fish and sauce in the steamer and steam over high heat for 15 to 20 minutes.

4. Transfer the fish to a long platter. Pour the sauce over the fish and serve hot.

NOTE: For those who do not like hot and spicy dishes, the dried red peppers can be omitted. Or the dish can be made somewhat milder by discarding the seeds when dicing the peppers.

Steamed Pearl Balls 珍珠肉丸

This impressive dish is one of the favorite dishes in our cooking school. After being steamed, the glutinous rice coating the meatballs becomes beautifully white and shining, and the balls resemble large pearls, hence the name.

This dish originated in Hupei, the province north of Hunan. The meatballs cooked this way are crunchy and succulent with chopped water chestnuts and mushrooms. They make excellent hors d'oeuvres and are especially beautiful when served directly from a bamboo steamer.

INGREDIENTS:
⅔ cup glutinous rice (sweet rice)
4 to 6 dried Chinese mushrooms
1 lb (500 g) ground pork
1 egg
1¼ tsp salt
¼ tsp sugar
1 Tbs light soy sauce
1 Tbs tapioca starch dissolved in 2 Tbs water
6 to 8 fresh water chestnuts, peeled and finely chopped
1 stalk scallion, finely chopped

PROCEDURES:
1. Rinse and then soak the glutinous rice for at least 3 hours. Drain the rice and spread it out on a cloth towel to dry (about 30 minutes).

2. Soak the mushrooms in hot water for about 20 minutes. Cut off and discard stems. Chop the mushrooms fine.

3. In a mixing bowl, combine the ground pork, egg, salt, sugar, soy sauce, and the tapioca starch and water mixture. Mix well, then add finely chopped water chestnuts, mushrooms, and scallion, and mix some more.

4. Scoop up about 1½ Tbs. of the pork mixture with a wet hand and shape it into a ball about 1 inch (2.5 cm) in diameter. Evenly roll one ball at a time on the rice, then place the ball directly on a lightly oiled steamer rack. Cover and refrigerate until ready to steam.

TO COOK:
5. Steam the pearl balls (about 30) over medium-high heat for 20 to 25 minutes. Serve hot.

NOTE: For those who prefer, ground veal or beef can be used but the taste will not be as good. The Steamed Pearl Balls can be frozen for future use. Just defrost then heat them up by steaming for about 15 minutes. They are excellent hors d'oeuvres or can be served as one of the main courses.

Spicy Shredded Beef with Cellophane Noodles 乾扁牛肉絲

Chungking, a major city in the Szechuan province, is where this tasty hot and spicy dish originated. The Chinese call it Dry-Cooked Shredded Beef, and it is easy to understand why. The beef is stir-fried for quite some time (at least 5 minutes) until the moisture is "baked" away by the high heat of the wok, and the meat acquires a unique, chewy texture and a concentrated flavor. The taste is all in the beef and vegetables since this dish has no sauce at all. You need to eat slowly in order to savor the full flavor. Spicy Shredded Beef is also very colorful to serve; its shredded red carrots, green celery, and dark-brown beef strips contrast beautifully with the bed of white crispy noodles. Rice noodles can be used instead of cellophane noodles.

INGREDIENTS:

1 lb (500 g) flank steak or any beef steak
3 Tbs dark soy sauce
1 Tbs Chinese rice wine } *to marinate beef*
2 tsp sugar
1 oz (30 g) cellophane noodles (bean thread)
2 cups peanut or vegetable oil
2 cups celery, shredded
2 cups carrots, shredded
2 tsp dried red pepper, chopped
1 tsp ginger root, finely chopped
1 tsp sesame oil

PROCEDURES:

1. First cut the beef into ⅛-inch-thick (3-mm) slices. Then shred the slices into 2-inch-long (5-cm) strips. Marinate with soy sauce, wine, and sugar for 30 minutes.

2. Cut the cellophane noodles into shorter lengths and loosen them. Deep-fry them in 2 cups very hot oil, about 400° F (204° C), for 5 seconds on both sides. Crush the noodles into smaller pieces and lay them in one thin layer on a platter.

TO COOK:

3. Heat a wok and add 2 Tbs of the used oil. Stir-fry the shredded celery and carrots for 2 minutes. Remove.

4. Heat 3 Tbs oil in wok. Add the chopped dried red pepper and ginger first, then the beef. Stir over high heat for about 5 minutes until the liquid drains from the beef. Continue to stir-fry over high heat until the liquid is completely evaporated and the beef strips are dry and dark in color. Add the cooked celery and carrots; mix well. Garnish with sesame oil; mix again.

5. Place the beef and vegetable mixture over the fried cellophane noodles. Serve hot.

NOTE: The cellophane noodles can be deep-fried ahead of time and kept in a large glass jar or on a plate covered with plastic wrap. The shredded beef and shredded vegetables can also be cooked totally ahead of time and kept warm in the oven for about half an hour. Just before serving, pour the beef and vegetables over the fried noodles and serve.

Fish-Flavored Chicken 魚香鷄絲

This elegant dish has a delicately hot, as well as a sweet and sour, taste. No fish is used to flavor this dish; it is called "Fish-Flavored Chicken" because its sauce is usually used to cook fish. Since the province of Szechuan is located in the mountainous inland region of China, fish is not readily available. Therefore, people often use chicken or pork as a substitute. The beautifully shredded chicken, served on a bed of green snow peas, is coated with the light-brown glazed sauce. It is an excellent main dish to serve when you entertain.

INGREDIENTS:
1 whole chicken breast or chicken cutlet
½ egg white ⎫
½ tsp salt ⎬ to marinate chicken
1 Tbs Chinese rice wine ⎪
1 tsp tapioca starch ⎭
½ lb (250 g) fresh snow peas
¼ tsp dried red pepper, chopped ⎫
1 Tbs light soy sauce ⎪
1 Tbs Chinese rice wine ⎬ combined seasoning sauce
1 tsp sugar ⎪
1 tsp white rice vinegar ⎪
1 tsp tapioca starch ⎭
7 Tbs peanut or vegetable oil
½ tsp sugar
½ tsp salt
1 Tbs Chinese rice wine
2 tsp ginger root, finely minced
1 stalk scallion, finely chopped
1 clove garlic, chopped

PROCEDURES:
1. Slice the chicken into slices ⅛ inch (3 mm) thick and about 2 inches (5 cm) long, then shred the slices into strips 2 inches (5 cm) long. Marinate with egg white, salt, wine, and tapioca starch for at least 30 minutes.

2. Rinse and then shred the snow peas. Combine the sauce ingredients in a small bowl.

TO COOK:
3. Heat 2 Tbs oil in wok. Stir-fry the shredded snow peas for a few seconds. Then season with ½ tsp sugar and ½ tsp salt and splash in the rice wine. Mix well. Dish out to a serving plate.

4. Heat the wok very hot; add 5 Tbs oil, then stir in the shredded chicken. Stir-fry until the chicken separates into pieces. Remove chicken with a strainer.

5. Heat the same wok with the remaining oil. Add the ginger, scallion, and garlic. Stir-fry for a few seconds, then add the cooked chicken. Mix the sauce mix-

ture well and pour over the chicken. Stir over high heat until it coats the chicken with a clear glaze. Dish onto the snow peas. Serve hot.

NOTE: The final cooking time is short, and this dish is best when served as a last-minute, stir-fried dish. Watercress can be used instead of snow peas.

(*Top*) Stir-Fried Diced Chicken in Bird's Nest

(*Bottom*) Stuffed Bean Curd, Cantonese Style

**Sautéed Mixed
Vegetables**

Scallops and Chinese Radish Balls

**Stir-Fried Lovers'
Shrimp**

Dry-Cooked String Beans

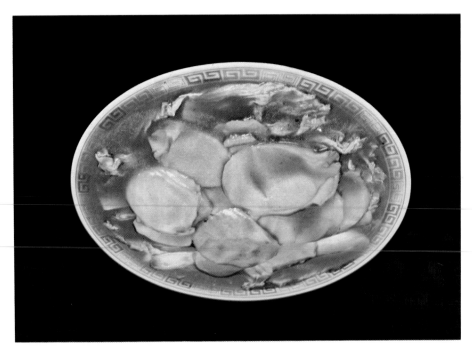

Abalone in Oyster Sauce

Squirrel Fish

Braised Soy Sauce Chicken

Chinese Fire Pot with Assorted Meats and Vegetables

**Quail Eggs in
Brown Sauce**

Fried Dumplings

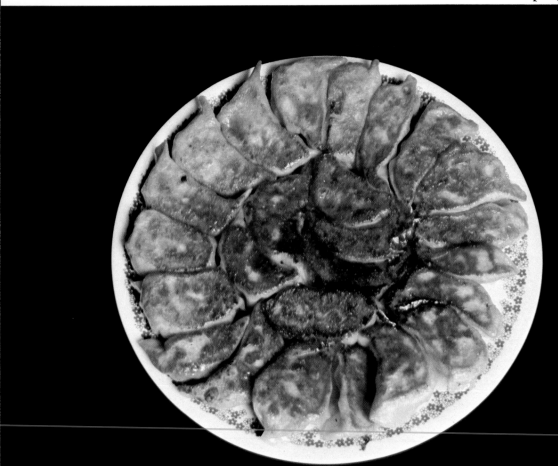

Yangchow Fried Rice

Seafood Sizzling Rice

Fish-Flavored Chicken

Spicy Shredded Beef with Cellophane Noodles

Shredded Pork (or Beef) in Hot Sauce 魚香肉絲

The Chinese also call this dish "Fish-Flavored Shredded Pork." But the sauce used here is very different from the "fish-flavored" sauce used to cook Fish-Flavored Chicken (see the previous recipe). The shredded meat here is coated with a dark brown glazed sauce, and the dash of Chin Kiang vinegar gives it a seductive aroma. Crunchy tree ears and water chestnuts are used to contrast with the soft-textured meat. In Chinese restaurants here, this dish is often named "Shredded Meat in Garlic Sauce," because the restaurateurs know that a dish named "fish-flavored" may not appeal to Americans.

INGREDIENTS:

1 lb (500 g) boneless pork loin or 4 pork chops
2 Tbs dark soy sauce ⎫
1 Tbs Chinese rice wine ⎬ to marinate pork
½ tsp sugar ⎪
1 Tbs tapioca starch ⎭
2 Tbs tree ears
6 to 8 fresh water chestnuts
2 Tbs dark soy sauce ⎫
1 Tbs Chinese rice wine ⎪
½ tsp salt ⎪
1 Tbs sugar ⎪
½ Tbs Chin Kiang vinegar ⎬ combined seasoning sauce
2 Tbs hot bean sauce ⎪
2 tsp tapioca starch ⎪
1 Tbs sesame oil ⎪
½ tsp black pepper ⎪
2 stalks scallions, shredded ⎭
5 Tbs peanut or vegetable oil
2 tsp ginger root, chopped
1 tsp garlic, chopped

PROCEDURES:

1. Slice the pork into thin slices; then shred them into thin strips 2 inches (5 cm) long. Marinate the meat with the soy sauce, wine, sugar, and tapioca starch for 15 to 20 minutes.

2. Soak the tree ears in hot water for about 20 minutes. Cut or break them into smaller pieces. Peel the fresh water chestnuts. Slice and then shred them into strips.

3. Mix all the combined seasoning sauce ingredients in a bowl.

TO COOK:

4. Heat 4 Tbs oil in a wok. Stir-fry the shredded pork for 2 minutes. Remove with a strainer and set aside.

5. Heat another 1 Tbs oil in the wok. Stir-fry the chopped ginger and garlic, then add the tree ears and water chestnuts. Stir a few times; mix in the shredded pork, stirring constantly. Finally pour in the combined seasoning sauce, mix well, and serve hot.

NOTE: Beef can be used instead of pork. This dish can be kept warm in the oven for about 10 to 15 minutes, but it is always best when served immediately after stir-frying.

Shrimps, Szechuan Style 乾燒蝦仁

This dish is also called Dry-Cooked Shrimps, Szechuan Style. In contrast to the delicate-looking Shrimp in Lobster Sauce (page 136), the sauce in this dish is all but absorbed, and the flavor of the shrimp is deliciously hot. This dish is also beautifully red with speckles of green chopped scallions. It is a rather fast dish to make. For those who are found of hot and spicy dishes, this may be a good dish to try.

INGREDIENTS:

1 lb (500 g) fresh or frozen raw, shrimps, peeled and deveined
1 Tbs tomato catsup
1 Tbs chili sauce
1 Tbs Chinese rice wine
1 Tbs dark soy sauce   } combined seasoning sauce
1 tsp sugar
½ tsp salt
¼ tsp dried red pepper, chopped
1 Tbs tapioca starch
2 Tbs peanut or vegetable oil
4 stalks scallions, chopped
2 Tbs ginger root, chopped
2 cloves garlic, chopped

PROCEDURES:

1. Defrost the shrimps. Rinse and drain, then thoroughly pat them dry with paper towels.

2. Mix tomato catsup, chili sauce, wine, soy sauce, sugar, salt, dried red pepper, and tapioca starch in a bowl to make the combined seasoning sauce.

TO COOK:

3. Heat oil in the wok. Add scallions, ginger, and garlic and stir for about ½ minute. Drop in shrimps and stir constantly for about 2 minutes or until the shrimps change color.

4. Pour in half of the combined seasoning sauce. Stir a few times, then pour in the rest of the sauce. Stir a few more times. Serve hot.

Steamed Spareribs with Spicy Rice Powder 粉蒸排骨

Steaming is the most delicate and least demanding of all Chinese cooking techniques. Steaming also intensifies the tastes when the ingredients are seasoned with marinade. In this dish, the spareribs are first marinated to absorb flavor and then coated with the spicy rice powder before steaming. The result is spectacular! The spareribs become tender and moist, with a subtle spicy flavor. They are excellent hors d'oeuvres or can be served as one of the main dishes. If bamboo steamers are used, the spareribs should be served directly from these beautiful containers.

INGREDIENTS:
1 stalk scallion, shredded
⅛ tsp ground-roasted Szechuan peppercorn
⅛ tsp dried red pepper, chopped
2 Tbs dark soy sauce   } to marinate spareribs
1 Tbs Chinese rice wine
½ tsp salt
1 tsp sugar
1½ lbs (750 g) spareribs (ask your butcher to cut across bones into sections 1½ inches or 4 cm long)
⅔ cup spicy rice powder
bok choy leaves

PROCEDURES:
1. Mix the scallion, peppercorn, dried red pepper, soy sauce, wine, salt, and sugar in a mixing bowl. Stir well to dissolve the salt and sugar. Set aside.

2. Cut the spareribs between each rib. Wash and drain. Add to the bowl with the marinade and let stand for 20 to 30 minutes. Turn and mix several times when marinating.

3. Coat each sparerib with the spicy rice powder. Arrange with shredded scallion in a bamboo steamer lined with some bok choy leaves, making 2 layers at the most. Pour the extra marinade on top.

TO COOK:
4. Steam over medium-high heat for 1½ hours. Check after 1 hour of steaming; if some spicy rice powder coating the ribs is still dry, turn meat around and continue steaming until all the rice powder coating is moist, up to another half hour. Serve hot.

NOTE: Always check to see that there is enough water under the steamer. Have a kettle of boiling water ready on the stove to add to the steamer when it needs more water.

To make the ground-roasted Szechuan peppercorn: Stir about 4 Tbs of Szechuan peppercorns in a wok or saucepan, without oil, over medium heat for about 2 minutes or until they are lightly browned. Then crush the peppercorns to a fine powder and store it in a glass jar for future use.

Eggplant, Szechuan Style 魚香茄子

This Szechuan style eggplant dish is full of aroma and wonderful flavors. The eggplants, cooked soft and tender, gleam under a dark brown sauce with a hot spicy taste mingled with the sweet and sour flavor. It is an excellent dish to serve with plain rice or a milder meat or chicken dish.

INGREDIENTS:
4 small eggplants (about 1 lb or 500 g)
2 Tbs dark soy sauce
1 Tbs Chinese rice wine
1 tsp sugar } *combined seasoning sauce*
1 tsp salt
½ cup chicken broth
6 Tbs peanut or vegetable oil
1 tsp garlic, chopped
½ Tbs ginger root, chopped
1 Tbs hot bean sauce
½ Tbs Chin Kiang vinegar
1 Tbs sesame oil
1 stalk scallion, chopped

PROCEDURES:

1. Wash the eggplants and cut off the stalks. Without peeling, cut the eggplants into thumb-sized pieces about 2 inches (5 cm) long.

2. Combine the soy sauce, wine, sugar, salt, and chicken broth in a small bowl.

TO COOK:

3. Heat the oil in a wok, then turn to medium heat; stir-fry the eggplants until soft, about 4 to 5 minutes. Remove and set aside.

4. Stir-fry the chopped garlic and ginger for a few seconds; add the hot bean sauce and then add the combined seasoning sauce and bring to a boil. Add the eggplant and cook about 1 minute until the sauce is gone.

5. Add the vinegar and sesame oil; continue to stir-fry. Finally mix in the chopped scallion and serve.

NOTE: To cut down the final cooking time, the preparation can end at step 3, because the eggplant will need to be stir-fried again to warm it up. The finished dish can be covered and kept warm in the oven for about half an hour.

Bon Bon Chicken   棒棒鷄

This hot and spicy "cold mix" chicken salad dish is usually served either as one of the cold platters at a banquet or one of the main dishes in China. It is especially good for luncheon, and wonderful for picnics. When one of our cooking class students brought this dish to a picnic of 100 people, so many of these picnickers came to our school afterward and asked for this recipe that we soon ran out of copies!

The special combined seasoning sauce is what gives this dish its unique, exotic flavor, and the mung bean sheet and cucumber slices add a crunchy texture.

For those who do not like the hot peppery taste, the chili oil can be omitted.

INGREDIENTS:
1 whole skinned and boned chicken breast or chicken cutlet, uncooked
1 cucumber
2 dried mung bean sheets
2 Tbs sesame seed paste, diluted
*   with 2 Tbs warm water*
2 Tbs light soy sauce
½ tsp salt
2 tsp sugar
1 Tbs white rice vinegar
1 Tbs sesame oil   } *combined seasoning sauce*
1 Tbs hot chili oil (to taste)
¼ tsp Szechuan peppercorn,
*   roasted and ground to powder*
2 cloves garlic, finely chopped
2 stalks scallions, finely chopped
¼ cup Chinese parsley leaves

PROCEDURES:
1. Put the chicken in water (enough to cover) in a saucepan. Bring to a boil and then simmer for 5 minutes. Turn off the heat and let the chicken stay in the water until cool, about 15 minutes. Use your fingers to tear the chicken into long strips. Set aside.

2. Peel the cucumber and split lengthwise into 2 pieces. Remove the seeds and slice into thin pieces. Sprinkle with salt, toss, and let stand for 20 minutes.

3. Soak the mung bean sheets in boiling hot water for 10 minutes. Drain and cover with cold water. Leave in cold water until cool. Drain and cut into ½- by 2-inch (1.5- by 5-cm) rectangular pieces. Put in a serving dish.

4. Squeeze water from the cucumber and mix with the bean sheet slices. Then add the shredded chicken on top.

5. Dissolve sesame seed paste in 2 Tbs warm water. Add mixture to other sauce ingredients and mix into a smooth, thin sauce. Pour about half of this sauce on top of the chicken dish and serve the rest in a sauce bowl. Garnish the chicken with Chinese parsley leaves. Serve cold.

NOTE: This dish can be prepared ahead of time. Dried mung bean sheets, just like bean sprouts and cellophane noodles (bean threads), are made from mung beans. They must be soaked in boiling hot water for about 10 minutes until soft before you can use them in salads or for cooking. Agar-agar strips can be used instead of the bean sheets. But agar-agar should be cut and soaked in *cold* water, not hot water, for a few minutes. Drain and squeeze out excess water before use. For instructions on making ground-roasted Szechuan peppercorn, please see the recipe for Ma Po Bean Curd (page 90).

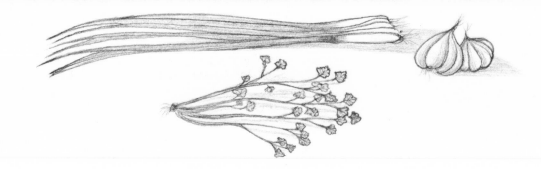

Dry-Cooked Prawns or Shrimps, Szechuan Style 乾燒明蝦

The Chinese believe that shrimps cooked in the shells have more flavor. They like to suck on the delicious shells before removing them with their teeth. To my surprise practically all of the students who have tried this recipe enjoyed it tremendously and did not mind removing the shells at the table at all. If you have never had shrimps served in the shells, do try this recipe.

INGREDIENTS:
1 lb (500 g) fresh large shrimps or prawns
3 Tbs tomato catsup
2 Tbs dark soy sauce
2 Tbs sugar
2 Tbs Chinese rice wine   } *combined seasoning sauce*
½ tsp tapioca starch
2 tsp fresh ginger root, minced
2 Tbs hot bean sauce
1 tsp sesame oil
2 stalks scallions, chopped
3 Tbs peanut or vegetable oil

PROCEDURES:
1. Devein the shrimps; wash and drain.
2. Mix the catsup, soy sauce, sugar, wine, tapioca starch, ginger, hot bean sauce and sesame oil to form the combined seasoning sauce.

TO COOK:
3. Heat oil in the wok. Fry the shrimps about 5 minutes on each side. When done, scoop in two-thirds of the combined seasoning sauce a little at a time and stir-fry until the sauce is absorbed by the shrimps. Pour in the final third of the sauce and mix thoroughly. Garnish with the chopped scallions. Serve immediately.

NOTE: For Dry-Cooked Shrimps, Shanghai Style, omit the hot bean sauce. Leftover shrimps are equally tasty when served cold.

Steamed Beef with Spicy Rice Powder 粉蒸牛肉

As mentioned before, steaming is the most delicate and least demanding of all Chinese cooking techniques. Steamed food is often tender, moist, tasty, and nutritious. This recipe is a marvelous Szechuan specialty. The spicy rice powder comes in plastic packages and is available in Chinese grocery stores. This dish can be served either as hors d'oeuvres or a main dish, and can be served directly from the bamboo steamers.

INGREDIENTS:

1 lb (500 g) beef steak or London broil
2 Tbs dark soy sauce ⎫
1½ Tbs Chinese rice wine
½ tsp salt
½ tsp sugar
1 Tbs hot bean sauce
2 stalks scallions, cut into 1-inch ⎬ to marinate beef
    (2.5 -cm) pieces
3 slices ginger root
1 star anise, ground
3 Tbs sesame oil ⎭
1 Tbs Szechuan peppercorn
bok choy leaves
¾ cup spicy rice powder

PROCEDURES:

1. Cut the beef into thin, 1½-inch-square (4-cm) slices. Marinate with soy sauce, wine, salt, sugar, hot bean sauce, scallion, ginger, star anise, and sesame oil for about half an hour.

2. Stir the Szechuan peppercorn in a wok without any oil for a few minutes until the aroma comes out. Pound into powder. Set aside.

3. Line the bamboo steamer rack with large bok choy leaves. Coat both sides of the beef with spicy rice powder. Arrange the beef slices on the bok choy leaves, making 2 layers at the most. Pour the extra marinade on top.

TO COOK:

4. First boil the water, then steam the beef over high heat for 20 to 30 minutes. Sprinkle some Szechuan peppercorn powder on the beef before serving.

Twice-Cooked Pork 回鍋肉

This famous Szechuan recipe involves boiling the pork first and then stir-frying it at the last minute. The authentic version recorded here uses fermented black beans, dried red pepper, and Chinese cabbage, though many people nowadays like to use sweet bean sauce and hot bean sauce in this dish. Spicy in taste and full of the rich flavors of the fermented black beans, garlic, and ginger, this dish is enjoyed by many Americans who like spiced food.

INGREDIENTS:
1 lb (500 g) boneless pork loin
2 cups water
1 Tbs Chinese rice wine
3 slices ginger root
½ cup bamboo shoots, winter
½ cup five-spiced brown bean curd
¼ lb (125 g) Chinese cabbage
4 Tbs peanut or vegetable oil
½ tsp salt
2 cloves garlic, crushed
¼ cup fermented black beans, minced
1 tsp dried red pepper, chopped
2 Tbs black soy sauce
¼ cup stock from cooking pork

PROCEDURES:

1. Boil the entire piece of pork in a pan with 2 cups of water, 1 Tbs Chinese rice wine, and 1 slice ginger for ½ hour. Cool thoroughly, then slice the pork into 1-inch-square (2.5-cm) pieces about ⅛ inch (3 mm) thick. Reserve the stock for later use.

2. Slice the winter bamboo shoots and five-spiced brown bean curd. Set aside on a plate. Cut Chinese cabbage into 1-inch-square (2.5-cm) pieces.

TO COOK:

3. Heat 2 Tbs oil in the wok. Add the salt, then the Chinese cabbage; stir constantly for one minute. Then add the bamboo shoot slices and the five-spiced brown bean curd. Mix well. Remove and spread on a plate.

4. Heat the remaining 2 Tbs oil in the wok. Add the remaining 2 slices of ginger, crushed garlic, and minced black beans and stir a few seconds. Then add the chopped red pepper and sliced pork. Stir and mix for 1 to 2 minutes. Pour in the soy sauce and ¼ cup of the reserved stock; stir and cook for 1 minute. Mix in the cooked cabbage, bamboo shoots, and brown bean curd and serve immediately.

NOTE: This dish can be stir-fried ahead of time and kept in a warm oven for about ½ hour.

Seafood Sizzling Rice 三鮮鍋巴

Sizzling rice is really "deep-fried rice crust" made with glutinous or long grain rice. When the deep-fried rice crust is dropped into hot soup, it makes a sizzling sound and emits steam. During World War II, in order to show patriotic feelings, people liked to call this dish "Bombard Tokyo."

This fancy dish is fun to serve. Tender and tasty crabmeat and abalone mushrooms, served on top of the crunchy sizzling rice, covered with a glistening, light-colored sauce, is enough to make everyone's mouth water.

INGREDIENTS:

½ lb (250 g) peeled and deveined frozen shrimps
1 Tbs Chinese rice wine ⎫
½ tsp salt ⎪
1 tsp tapioca starch ⎬ to marinate shrimp
½ egg white ⎭
¼ lb (125 g) fresh snow peas
6 fresh water chestnuts
1 can abalone mushrooms
1 cup canned crab or lobster meat
1 Tbs light soy sauce ⎫
1 Tbs Chinese rice wine ⎪
½ tsp salt ⎪
½ tsp sugar ⎪
⅛ tsp white pepper ⎬ combined seasoning sauce
½ cup chicken broth ⎪
2 Tbs tapioca starch ⎪
1 Tbs white rice vinegar ⎪
3 Tbs catsup ⎭
3 cups peanut or vegetable oil
6 cakes dried sizzling rice (2 inches or 5 cm square)

PROCEDURES:

1. Defrost and rinse the shrimps. Pat dry thoroughly with paper towels. Marinate with the above marinade.

2. String the snow peas, then parboil. Peel and slice water chestnuts.

3. Cut the abalone mushrooms into 1-inch (2.5 -cm) pieces. Put the mushrooms, snow peas, sliced water chestnuts, and crab or lobster meat on a plate.

4. Combine the sauce ingredients in a bowl to make the combined seasoning sauce.

TO COOK:

5. Heat 3 cups oil in the wok until very hot, about 400° F (204° C). Fry the dried sizzling rice, 2 pieces at a time, until light brown and crispy on both sides (about 10 seconds). Drain and set aside on a heatproof platter. Break into smaller pieces and keep warm in oven.

6. Heat 2 Tbs of the used oil over high heat. Add shrimps and stir-fry until they change color (about 1 minute). Remove and set aside.

7. Heat the wok with 2 Tbs of the used oil over moderate heat. Stir-fry the mushrooms, water chestnuts, and snow peas for ½ minute. Mix the combined sauce again and pour into the wok. Stir until the sauce thickens and forms a clear glaze. Turn heat to high and add the crab or lobster meat and cooked shrimps; mix thoroughly. Pour into a shallow serving bowl.

8. Take the hot fried sizzling rice out of the oven. Pour the cooked seafood and vegetables over the rice. Serve immediately.

NOTE: Abalone mushrooms, a new variety, are close in taste, texture, and color to the abalone. They are available at Oriental food stores.

Stuffed Eggplant 茄子餅

These deep-fried eggplant "sandwiches" are so delicious that it is hard to stop eating them. They are not only excellent hors d'oeuvres, but also can be served as a fancy vegetable dish. Furthermore, they are equally popular as snacks. The coating is crispy, the eggplant tender, and the filling delectable.

INGREDIENTS:

¼ cup dried shrimps
½ lb (250 g) ground pork
1 scallion, finely chopped
½ tsp salt
½ tsp sugar ⎫ filling
1 Tbs dark soy sauce
1 Tbs Chinese rice wine
¼ tsp pepper
1 Tbs tapioca starch ⎭
1 medium-size eggplant or 3 to 4 small ones (about 1 lb or 500 g)
1 egg, beaten
1 cup bread crumbs
2 cups peanut or vegetable oil

PROCEDURES:

1. Soak the dried shrimps in hot water for about 30 minutes. Drain and chop fine.

2. Combine the filling ingredients in a mixing bowl. Mix well and set aside.

3. Peel the eggplant and cut into slices ⅛ inch (3 mm) thick. Spread about 1 Tbs filling on one slice of eggplant and cover with another slice. Dip each stuffed sandwich in the beaten egg, then roll in the bread crumbs. Set aside on a plate.

TO COOK:

4. Heat the oil in a wok. Deep-fry a few coated eggplant pieces at a time for 2 minutes on each side or until brown. Serve hot.

NOTE: The fried eggplants can be reheated in a 350° F (177° C) oven for about 10 to 15 minutes.

Odd-Flavor Chicken 怪味鷄

There are several unique features of this delicious chicken dish. First of all, it is completely boneless; it can be served conveniently at buffet dinners or as hors d'oeuvres. Secondly, the cut-up chicken pieces are reassembled into the chicken shape and served with a light-brown sauce embellished with multi-colored ingredients. It is a very impressive dish to serve. Finally, the taste is beyond words.

The dish is called Odd-Flavor Chicken because it seems odd to combine and use such a great variety of sauces and ingredients. And yet when the proper amount of each ingredient is used, the result is spectacular! No wonder this dish has been called Millionaire Chicken—it tastes so good that it is thought to be worth a million dollars.

INGREDIENTS:

2 to 3 lb (1 to 1½ kg) chicken
1 Tbs Chinese rice wine
2 slices ginger root
4 Tbs light soy sauce ⎫
2 Tbs honey ⎪
1 Tbs Chinese rice wine ⎬ Group A sauce mix
2 cloves garlic, crushed ⎪
½ tsp salt ⎭
3 Tbs peanut or vegetable oil ⎫
2 stalks scallions, chopped ⎪
4 slices ginger root, minced ⎪
½ tsp Szechuan peppercorn, ⎬ Group B sauce mix
    roasted and crushed ⎪
¼ tsp dried red pepper, chopped ⎭
½ lb (250 g) Chinese cabbage

PROCEDURES:

1. Wash and clean the chicken. Boil 3 quarts of water in a large deep pan. Add 1 Tbs of Chinese rice wine and 2 slices of ginger. Submerge the chicken in the boiling water and continue boiling for 20 minutes. Turn off the heat and let the chicken cool in the water for at least 30 minutes before taking it out.

2. Combine the ingredients of Group A in a bowl and let stand for at least 5 minutes.

3. Combine and then heat the Group B ingredients in a small pan over low heat for about 3 minutes. Then pour this sauce into the bowl containing A. Mix well.

4. Shred and then arrange the Chinese cabbage on a large platter.

TO CUT AND REASSEMBLE THE CHICKEN:

5. When the chicken is cool enough to touch, place it on a chopping board. With a cleaver disjoint the wings and the legs (with thighs). Set aside. Now turn the body on its side, cut through it lengthwise so that the entire breast is separated

from the back. Now the chicken has been cut into 6 pieces (2 wings, 2 legs with thighs, 1 back, and 1 breast). First remove bones carefully from the back and breast; then remove bones from the legs with thighs. Leave the wings untouched. While removing bones from the back and breast is a relatively easy process, it is more difficult to remove them from the rest of the chicken and not easy to describe here. However, with practice you will soon develop the correct technique.

6. First chop the entire back piece crosswise into 1-inch-wide (2.5-cm) rectangular pieces. Arrange them in the center of the platter on the shredded cabbages. Then cut the entire breast the same way into 1-inch-wide (2.5-cm) pieces. Place them on top of the back pieces. Cut each wing at one joint (into 2 pieces) and place them at each side of the body. Finally chop the leg with thigh crosswise into 4 to 5 pieces and place them at their respective places at the lower sides of the body.

7. Pour the warm sauce over all of the chicken and serve at room temperature or cold.

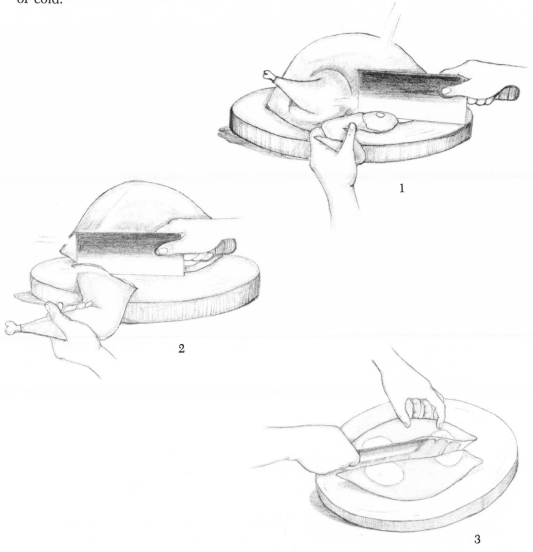

1

2

3

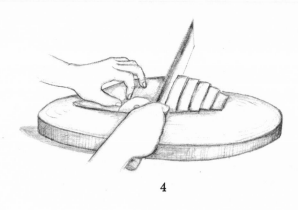

4

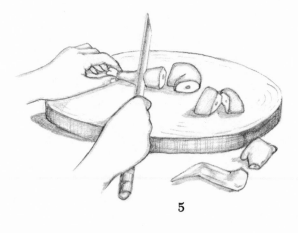

5

6

NOTE: This dish can be prepared beforehand. The chicken can be cooked the day before, then refrigerated. Cut the chicken an hour or so before dinner time, arrange the pieces on cabbage leaves and leave it in the refrigerator. The two groups of ingredients for the sauce can be assembled and placed in a bowl and saucepan, respectively. The final preparation takes but a few minutes. Since the dish can be served cold, it is an especially good dish for summer.

Orange-Flavor Beef   陳皮牛

This is a very pretty dish: tender beef slices submerged in a gleaming dark brown sauce served on a bed of crisp green bok choy. The flavors are manifold and yet not conflicting. The initial taste is peppery hot; then the deep citrus flavor of the orange peel emerges, followed by the gingery taste and the stimulating aroma from the Chin Kiang vinegar. The zestful taste of this dish lingers long after you finish eating!

INGREDIENTS:

1 lb (500 g) flank steak or other beef steak
1 lb (500 g) bok choy
2 Tbs dark soy sauce ⎫
1 Tbs Chinese rice wine ⎬ to marinate sliced beef
1 Tbs tapioca starch ⎭
10 Tbs peanut or vegetable oil
½ tsp salt
¼ tsp sugar
½ Tbs Chinese rice wine
1½ Tbs dark soy sauce ⎫
1 Tbs Chinese rice wine ⎪
¼ tsp salt ⎪
½ Tbs sugar ⎪
½ Tbs Chin Kiang dark vinegar ⎬ combined seasoning sauce
1 Tbs hot bean sauce ⎪
1 Tbs sesame oil ⎪
1 tsp tapioca starch ⎭
2 stalks scallions, chopped
2 tsp ginger, chopped
6 to 8 pieces dried orange peel, 1 inch (2½ cm) square
8 to 10 dried red peppers, whole
½ tsp salt
¼ tsp sugar

PROCEDURES:

1. When flank steak is used, first cut with the grain into three long strips each about 2 inches (5 cm) wide. Then cut the beef across the grain into very thin slices, at least ⅛ inch (3 mm), and about 2 inches (5 cm) long and ½ inch (1.5 cm) wide. (When other steaks are used, it is not absolutely necessary to cut this way, but the same cutting method can be followed.) Marinate with the above marinade.

2. Wash the bok choy, and then cut the leaves and stalks into 1-inch (2.5-cm) pieces. Boil a pot of water; drop in the bok choy pieces and continue to boil for about 1 minute. Rinse thoroughly with cold water. Drain and set aside.

3. Combine the ingredients listed above to make the combined seasoning sauce.

4. Stir-fry bok choy in 2 Tbs oil for about ½ minute. Sprinkle ½ tsp salt, ¼ tsp sugar, and rice wine. Mix well and place on a serving dish.

5. Heat 4 Tbs oil in a wok over high heat. Mix another 2 Tbs oil into the beef to loosen it. Stir-fry the beef until it changes color (not over 2 minutes). Remove and set aside.

6. Heat 2 Tbs oil in wok. Sauté the scallion, ginger, orange peel, and dried red peppers for about ½ minute. Add beef to the wok, stir well, then pour in the well-stirred combined seasoning sauce. Mix and stir over high heat for a few seconds. Put on top of the bok choy and serve hot.

NOTE: Snow peas or watercress can be used instead of bok choy.

Crispy Spicy Fish 脆皮魚

As mentioned before, fish is a symbol of abundance and is often served whole as the finale of a banquet to signify that there will still be plenty of food in the coming year.

Water chestnut flour and tapioca starch are used to coat this fish before deep-frying so that the crust will be exceptionally light. Chinese rice wine is used to diminish the fishiness and to bring out the flavor, while the wine rice (fermented rice) is used to create a deeper wine taste and a thicker consistency. The end result is a delectable, crispy fish, stimulatingly hot and yet refreshingly light.

INGREDIENTS:

1½ to 2 lb (750 g to 1 kg) whole sea bass, striped bass, sea trout, or quick frozen
Chinese yellow croaker, with head and tail
¼ cup tapioca starch
¼ cup water chestnut flour
¼ cup dried Chinese mushrooms
½ cup wine rice (fermented rice)
⅓ cup Chinese rice wine
2 Tbs dark soy sauce
2 Tbs hot bean sauce

} *combined seasoning sauce*

6 cups peanut or vegetable oil
2 whole dried red peppers, coarsely chopped
4 cloves garlic, chopped
¾ cup scallions, chopped
3 Tbs ginger root, finely chopped
⅓ cup bamboo shoots, chopped
1 tsp tapioca starch dissolved in 2 Tbs water

PROCEDURES:

1. Clean the fish and dry well with paper towels. Cut diagonal slashes ¾ inch (1 cm) apart almost to the bone on both sides of the fish. Mix the tapioca starch and water chestnut flour; dredge the fish in this mixture to cover the entire surface of the fish. Rub mixture into the slashes, over the top, and inside the fish. Set fish aside.

2. Soak the mushrooms in hot water until soft. Remove the stems and chop fine. Combine the sauce ingredients.

TO COOK:

3. Heat a large wok, add the oil, and heat until very hot. Lifting the fish by the tail, dip the fish into the hot oil, lift up, and dip again. Then lay fish down in the oil. After a few minutes, ladle the hot oil over the top of the fish. When the fish looks crisp and golden, bubbles cease to form on top of the oil, and the sizzling noise stops, the fish is done. Transfer the fish to a platter. (You can prepare the fish up to this point ahead of time and leave it at room temperature. Save the wok with the oil; the fish will have to be refried.)

4. A few minutes before serving, heat another wok or pan. Add 3 Tbs of the used oil. Add the dried red peppers and garlic, then the scallions. Stir-fry for 1 minute. Add the ginger, mushrooms, bamboo shoots, and the sauce mixture. Stir and cook for 1 more minute. Mix the tapioca starch and water well; pour over the sauce and stir until it thickens and forms a clear glaze. Keep warm on the stove.

5. Heat the wok with the used frying oil until it is very hot and refry the fish for about 3 to 4 minutes. Place the fried fish upright on its belly on a serving platter. With a towel, hold and press down gently on the neck of the fish so that the slashed belly sides protrude. Pour the hot sauce over the fish. Serve hot.

PART IV

Dishes Typical of Southern China (Canton)

Roast Pork Lomein 义烧捞麵

This well-known Cantonese lomein dish is simple, delicious, and nutritious. Many foods have special meanings to the Chinese, and noodles are no exception. Noodles are a symbol of longevity and therefore a must for birthdays. To signify a wish of long life for the celebrant, these noodles are never cut. The Chinese do not celebrate birthdays every year, but do celebrate every decade. Birthday parties are also held for the one-month-olds and the one-year-olds. Since the Chinese venerate old age, feeling that added years denote added wisdom, birthday parties are held to be more important for the old than for the young.

INGREDIENTS:

½ lb (250 g) precooked Chinese roast pork
½ lb (250 g) Chinese cabbage
½ lb (250 g) fresh bean sprouts
1 lb (500 g) lomein noodle (egg noodle)
3 Tbs peanut or vegetable oil
1 stalk scallion, cut into 2-inch (5-cm) pieces
1 Tbs dark soy sauce
½ tsp salt
2 Tbs oyster sauce

PROCEDURES:

1. Slice and then shred the roast pork into strips 2 inches (5 cm) long. Wash and then shred the Chinese cabbage. Rinse the bean sprouts with cold water.

2. Chop the noodle in half. Freeze half of it and add the other half to boiling water; boil for about 2 minutes. Drain and rinse with cold water. Drain well and mix with 1 Tbs of oil. Set aside.

TO COOK:

3. Heat 2 Tbs oil in the wok. Stir-fry the scallion and roast pork over high heat for about 1 minute. Add the Chinese cabbage and bean sprouts; mix well.

4. Spread the noodle on top of the vegetable and roast pork mixture. Sprinkle the soy sauce, salt, and oyster sauce on the noodle. Mix and toss over high heat for a few minutes. Serve hot.

NOTE: The final cooking time is only a few minutes, but the preparation (steps 1 and 2) should be done beforehand if possible and the ingredients kept refrigerated. The finished dish can be covered and kept warm in the oven for about ½ hour.

Chicken and Chinese Sausage Rice 鷄肉腊腸飯

This fancy and delicious rice dish is enjoyed tremendously by children and adults alike. It can be served as a snack or a side dish.

Chinese sausages are one of the foodstuffs that the Chinese always try to keep on hand for unexpected guests. In China you do not need to call first in order to visit your friends or relatives. You simply drop in. To show hospitality and appreciation for the guest's coming, the host and hostess often invite the guest to stay for lunch or dinner. Thus the sausages are extremely handy to have as an extra dish or to be combined with vegetables. Just place them on a plate and steam for 15 to 20 minutes, then cut each diagonally into long thin slices and serve. They are delicious and also add color to fried rice, stir-fried noodles, or vegetables. In America sliced Chinese sausages are often served as hors d'oeuvres—either alone or on crackers.

These sausages keep well for a month in the refrigerator and indefinitely in the freezer.

INGREDIENTS:

1 chicken cutlet or whole chicken breast
1 stalk scallion, cut into 1-inch
    (2.5-cm) pieces
2 slices ginger root
1 Tbs Chinese rice wine   } to marinate chicken
3 Tbs dark soy sauce
½ tsp salt
½ tsp sugar
2 Chinese sausages
4 to 6 dried Chinese mushrooms
2 cups long grain rice

PROCEDURES:

1. Using a cleaver, cut the chicken into 1- by 1½-inch (2.5- by 4-cm) pieces. Marinate the chicken slices for at least ½ hour in the scallion, ginger, wine, soy sauce, salt, and sugar marinade.

2. Slice the sausages diagonally into ¼-inch (1-cm) pieces.

3. Soak the mushrooms in hot water for about 20 minutes. Cut off and discard the stems. Cut each mushroom into 2 to 4 pieces.

TO COOK:

4. Rinse the rice once under cold water and drain well. Place it in a casserole, add 3 cups of water and bring to a boil. Without covering let it boil for about 5 minutes or until about 80% of the water has been absorbed. Arrange the sausage, chicken, and mushrooms over the rice and pour the marinade over the rice, discarding the scallion and ginger. Cover, turn to low heat and simmer for 20 minutes. Remove from heat and allow the rice to stand for at least 20 minutes before

serving. Loosen the rice, mix well so that the color of the rice is evenly brown. Transfer to a shallow serving bowl and serve hot.

5. If you use an electric rice cooker, put the rice and the amount of water specified in the rice cooker instructions in the cooker. Cover and press the button to start. After about 10 minutes when 80% of the water has been absorbed, arrange the sausage, chicken, mushrooms, and marinating sauce over the rice. Cover and continue cooking. When the button pops up, let the rice stand for at least 20 minutes before serving. Mix well and transfer into a serving bowl and serve hot.

NOTE: Leftover rice with sausages and chicken can be warmed up by placing it in a shallow bowl and steaming for about 15 minutes.

Bean Curd with Straw Mushrooms 草菇豆腐

Simple and nutritious, this bean curd dish is glazed with a dark brown sauce and beautifully embellished with umbrella-shaped straw mushrooms. Inexpensive bean curd (*to fu*) is used throughout the Orient as a prime source of protein. Since it is soft-textured and bland, it combines well with many ingredients. Sprinkle some light soy sauce, sesame seed paste (diluted into a smooth paste first by mixing 1 Tbs sesame paste with 2 Tbs warm water), sesame oil, and chopped scallion on top, and it becomes a delicious and nutritious salad, excellent for summer meals.

Fresh bean curd should be soaked in cold water and refrigerated. Change the water every day and it will keep about a week.

INGREDIENTS:
4 cakes firm bean curd or 2 cakes soft bean curd
1 Tbs tapioca starch
one 15-oz (500-g) can straw mushrooms
2 Tbs peanut or vegetable oil
1 stalk scallion, cut into 1-inch (2.5-cm) pieces
1 Tbs dark soy sauce
1½ Tbs oyster sauce
¼ tsp salt
1 tsp sesame oil

PROCEDURES:
1. Cut the bean curd cakes into smaller cubes, about ½ inch (1.5 cm) square.
2. Mix the tapioca starch with 2 Tbs liquid from the canned mushrooms.

TO COOK:
3. Heat the oil in a wok and add the scallion. Stir a few seconds, then add the bean curd cubes. Add the soy sauce, oyster sauce, salt, and straw mushrooms; stir gently and cook for about 3 minutes. When the liquid from bean curd is almost dry, stir in the tapioca starch mixture until it thickens.
4. Garnish with sesame oil. Serve hot.

NOTE: The finished dish can be covered and kept warm in the oven for about half an hour.

Shrimp Fried Rice, Cantonese Style 廣州 蝦仁 炒飯

Cantonese style fried rice usually uses dark soy sauce for color and taste. Mild but tasty, this fried rice dish is excellent for buffet dinners or luncheon. Steamed and sliced Chinese sausages or diced roast pork can be mixed with the fried rice for added color and flavor.

INGREDIENTS:
½ lb (250 g) frozen peeled and deveined shrimps
1 Tbs Chinese rice wine ⎫
½ tsp salt ⎬ to marinate shrimp
1 tsp tapioca starch ⎭
2 or 3 eggs
¼ tsp salt
7 Tbs peanut or vegetable oil
2 stalks scallions, chopped
3½ cups cooked rice, cold
1½ Tbs dark soy sauce
1 cup fresh bean sprouts (rinsed in cold water and drained)

PROCEDURES:
1. Defrost the shrimps, rinse with cold water, and pat dry thoroughly with paper towels. Mix the shrimps with wine, salt, and tapioca starch. Set aside. Beat the eggs with ¼ tsp salt.

TO COOK:
2. Heat 2 Tbs oil in a wok over high heat. Stir in the marinated shrimps and stir-fry for about 1 minute until they change color. Remove and set aside.

3. Heat another 2 Tbs oil in the wok. Stir in the chopped scallions and then the eggs. Scramble and break the eggs into small pieces until quite dry. Remove and set aside.

4. Heat the last 3 Tbs oil in the wok. Add the rice; stir until it is separated, coated with oil, and warm. Add soy sauce; stir and mix well. Add the cooked shrimp, bean sprouts, and scrambled eggs. Stir constantly until the ingredients are well blended and thoroughly heated—about 2 to 3 minutes. Serve hot.

NOTE: If desired, a pinch of salt can be added to the rice in step 4. The finished dish can be covered and kept warm in the oven for about ½ hour.

Beef in Oyster Sauce with Snow Peas and Water Chestnuts 蠔油牛肉

Tender beef slices in savory oyster sauce contrast beautifully with the crunchy white fresh water chestnuts and crisp green fresh snow peas in this famous Cantonese dish.

When fresh water chestnuts are available, by all means get them instead of the canned ones. They are sweeter, crunchier, and so delicious that people can't resist popping them into their mouths while peeling them. In China they are eaten raw as snacks and people enjoy them better than cookies or candies. Children even make a game of seeing who can peel them fastest with their teeth.

INGREDIENTS:

1 lb (500 g) beef steak
2 Tbs oyster sauce ⎫
1 Tbs black soy sauce ⎪
1 Tbs Chinese rice wine ⎬ to marinate beef
½ tsp sugar ⎪
1 Tbs tapioca starch ⎭
½ lb (250 g) fresh snow peas
8 to 10 fresh water chestnuts
2 Tbs oyster sauce ⎫
1 Tbs Chinese rice wine ⎪
1 tsp sugar ⎬ combined seasoning sauce
½ tsp tapioca starch ⎪
1 tsp sesame oil ⎭
5 Tbs peanut or vegetable oil
¼ tsp salt
1 stalk scallion, cut into 1-inch (2.5-cm) pieces
2 slices ginger root

PROCEDURES:

1. Cutting across the grain, slice the beef into very thin pieces ½ inch (1.5 cm) wide and 2 inches (5 cm) long.

2. Marinate the sliced beef with the oyster sauce, soy sauce, wine, sugar, and tapioca starch and set aside.

3. Remove the stem and strings from the snow peas. Rinse and then parboil in a pot. Rinse in cold water until cool. Peel and slice the water chestnuts. Mix the ingredients for the combined seasoning sauce.

TO COOK:

4. Heat 1 Tbs oil in a wok over high heat. Add the salt first and then the snow peas, stirring constantly (about ½ minute). Remove the snow peas and spread on a plate.

5. In the same wok, add the remaining 4 Tbs of oil, scallion, and ginger root. Add the beef mixture and stir constantly until the beef is almost cooked (not over 2 minutes). Add the snow peas and water chestnuts and then the well-stirred combined seasoning sauce. Mix thoroughly. Serve hot.

NOTE: The preparations up to step 3 can be done ahead of time and the food kept refrigerated. The final stir-frying time is only 2 to 3 minutes. This dish is best when served as a last-minute, stir-fried dish.

Chicken Velvet Corn Soup 鷄茸玉米湯

As mentioned before, soup, instead of tea or water, is served throughout a meal in China. Generally, no meal is served without a soup. A large soup tureen is placed in the center of the table with many other dishes of food surrounding it, and the diners spoon some soup to their own bowls throughout the meal.

This is a delicate, creamy soup, speckled with minced Smithfield ham for accent. Though often served at banquets, it is quite easy to prepare this soup at home.

INGREDIENTS:
1 whole skinned and boned chicken breast or cutlet, uncooked
3 egg whites
one 8-oz (250-g) can creamed corn
3 cups chicken broth
1 cup water
¼ tsp salt
2 Tbs tapioca starch dissolved in 3 Tbs water
2 Tbs Smithfield ham, cooked and minced

PROCEDURES:

1. Slice and mince the chicken. Mix well with 1 egg white and creamed corn; set aside.

2. Beat the remaining 2 egg whites and set aside.

TO COOK:

3. Bring the chicken broth and 1 cup water to a boil; add ¼ tsp salt. Then add the chicken and corn mixture and boil for 2 minutes. Add predissolved tapioca starch, stirring continuously until soup is thickened.

4. Reduce to low heat; add the beaten egg white slowly and stir until blended.

5. Pour into serving bowl and sprinkle with minced ham.

NOTE: Canned crab meat can be used instead of chicken to make Crab Velvet Corn Soup.

String Beans with Fermented Bean Curds 腐乳四季豆

Fu ju is fermented bean curd preserved in salt, wine, and water. The bean curd is first steamed, then fermented before it is bottled. It has the texture of very soft cheese but is much saltier. When used to flavor vegetables or meats, *fu ju* adds zest to the dishes. It can also be served right from the jar or can with congee or rice to whet the appetite. Generally only a small amount is used because it is quite salty.

INGREDIENTS:

1 lb (500 g) Chinese long beans (pole beans) or fresh young string beans
2 cakes fu ju *(fermented bean curd)*
1½ Tbs sauce from the fu ju *jar or can*
½ tsp sugar
½ cup cold water
2 Tbs peanut or vegetable oil
½ tsp salt

PROCEDURES:

1. Cut the beans into 2-inch (5-cm) pieces. Wash and drain.

2. Mash 2 cakes of *fu ju* with 1½ Tbs *fu ju* sauce in a small bowl. Then add sugar and water. Mix well and set aside.

TO COOK:

3. Heat 2 Tbs oil in the wok and stir-fry the green beans until all the beans are coated with oil. Add salt and mix well.

4. Add the mashed *fu ju* and mix a few times. After it begins to boil, turn heat to medium, cover and cook for 6 to 8 minutes. Serve warm.

NOTE: *Fu ju* may be used in place of salt to cook broccoli, spinach, and other greens.

Steamed Fish with Fermented Black Beans 豆豉蒸魚

Most Chinese are very fond of fish and seafood dishes, not only because seafood is abundant in China but also because it is delicious and nutritious. Fish are usually cooked whole, either steamed, red-cooked, or fried. Steamed fish is usually a family-style dish, easy to make yet tasty and pretty. This dish is full of the rich flavor of fermented black beans, ginger, and scallions. Any "fishy" taste is removed by rice wine. The final product is a delicate, juicy fish, full of aroma and flavor, and color-fully studded with speckles of fermented black beans and green scallions.

INGREDIENTS:

1½ lb (750 g) *whole sea bass, sea trout, red snapper, or flounder*
1 tsp salt
1 Tbs. salted black beans (fermented
    black beans), coarsely chopped
1 stalk scallion, cut into 2-inch-long
    (5-cm) pieces
1 Tbs ginger root, shredded   } *combined seasoning sauce*
½ tsp sugar
1 Tbs Chinese rice wine
1 Tbs light soy sauce
1 Tbs peanut or vegetable oil

PROCEDURES:

    1. Clean and wash the fish, pat dry with paper towels. Slash crosswise on both sides of the fish at 1½-inch (4-cm) intervals. Rub salt on both the inside and the outside of the fish and place it in a shallow bowl. (If the fish is too long for the bowl, cut it in half vertically to steam. Restore it to its original length after steaming.)

    2. Mix the sauce ingredients in a bowl. Pour this mixture all over the fish.

TO COOK:

    3. First boil the water. Then place the fish and the bowl on the steaming rack. Cover tightly and steam over high heat for about 20 minutes. Remove the bowl and transfer the fish and sauce to a larger platter. Serve hot.

NOTE: The preparation can be done ahead of time through step 2. Keep the fish and sauce refrigerated until ready to steam.

Winter Melon with Ham Soup 火腿冬瓜湯

Delicate, light, and flavorful, this soup is enjoyed tremendously by the Chinese. Winter melon is supposed to have medicinal value, and a bowl of winter melon soup is often taken for indigestion or illness. The melon is round or oval in shape with green skin, and the pulp inside is firm and white. After cooking the pulp becomes tender, soft, and translucent.

INGREDIENTS:
4 to 6 dried Chinese mushrooms
1 lb (500 g) winter melon
¼ lb (125 g) Smithfield ham, sliced (raw)
2 cups water
2 cups chicken broth
2 slices ginger root

PROCEDURES:
1. Soak the dried mushrooms in hot water for about 15 minutes. Cut off and discard the stems. Cut each mushroom into quarters.

2. Peel the green skin off the melon. Discard the seeds and cut off the soft part next to seeds. Wash, drain, and cut into slices about ¼ inch (6 mm) thick and 1 inch (2.5 cm) long.

3. Cut the Smithfield ham into thin slices ½ inch (1.5 cm) wide by 1 inch (2.5 cm) long.

TO COOK:
4. Add the sliced winter melon and Chinese mushrooms to 2 cups of water and 2 cups of chicken broth in a saucepan; bring to a boil. Then reduce the heat to low, half cover the saucepan, and simmer for 20 minutes until the melon is translucent and tender. Add the ham and ginger and cook for another 10 minutes. Serve hot.

NOTE: This soup can be cooked ahead of time and left on the stove. Heat before serving.

Beef and Broccoli in Oyster Sauce 蠔油芥蘭牛肉

Simple yet very pretty, this well-known Cantonese dish is also very tasty. The oyster sauce is a Cantonese seasoning; it gives a subtle "meat" flavor to a dish. Though made of oyster extract and other ingredients, it does not give any "fishy" taste; rather, it strengthens the flavor.

INGREDIENTS:
1 lb (500 g) beef steak (or flank steak)
2 Tbs oyster sauce ⎫
1 Tbs dark soy sauce ⎪
1 Tbs Chinese rice wine ⎬ to marinate beef
½ tsp sugar ⎪
1 Tbs tapioca starch ⎭
¾ lb (375 g) Chinese or regular broccoli
2 Tbs oyster sauce ⎫
1 Tbs Chinese rice wine ⎪
1 tsp sugar ⎬ combined seasoning sauce
½ tsp tapioca starch ⎪
1 tsp sesame oil ⎭
6 Tbs peanut or vegetable oil
1 tsp sugar
½ tsp salt
½ Tbs Chinese rice wine
1 stalk scallion, cut into 1-inch (2.5-cm) pieces
5 slices ginger root

PROCEDURES:
1. Cutting across the grain, slice the beef into very thin slices ½ inch (1.5 cm) wide and 2 inches (5 cm) long. Marinate with oyster sauce, soy sauce, wine, sugar, and tapioca starch for about half an hour.

2. Rinse the broccoli and peel off the tough skin. First cut off the flowerets; then, using the roll-cut method, cut the stems into pieces 1 inch (2.5 cm) long. Drop the broccoli flowerets and stems into boiling water for about 2 minutes, then remove and rinse with cold water. Set aside.

3. Mix the combined seasoning sauce ingredients.

TO COOK:
4. Heat 2 Tbs oil in wok, stir-fry the broccoli for a few seconds; add sugar, salt, and wine. Mix well, then remove and lay on plate.

5. Heat 4 Tbs oil in wok. Drop in the scallion and ginger slices, stir-fry for a few seconds. Add the beef, stir quickly and constantly until the beef is almost cooked (not over 2 minutes). Add the combined seasoning sauce, mix well, then remove and pour over broccoli and serve.

NOTE: Asparagus can be used instead of broccoli.

Shrimp with Cashew Nuts 腰果蝦仁

The Chinese feel that their cooking methods yield more delicate and tasty seafood than Western methods. They never boil shrimps which they feel makes them tough and tasteless. As this recipe demonstrates, shrimps are often first marinated and then quickly stir-fried over high heat. The end result is a crunchy shrimp dish, beautiful to look at and delicious to taste.

This dish is often served as the second course at a banquet. It is light, mild, and refreshing. The emphasis is on natural flavor, color, and texture. It is an excellent dish to serve when you entertain because the cooking time is extremely short. It also goes well with other spicy dishes.

INGREDIENTS:

1 lb (500 g) peeled and deveined shrimps, uncooked
1 egg white
1 Tbs tapioca starch
1 tsp salt   } to marinate shrimps
1 Tbs Chinese rice wine
2 Tbs Chinese rice wine
¼ tsp salt   } combined seasoning sauce
2 tsp sesame oil
¼ lb (125 g) cashew nuts, raw
8 Tbs peanut or vegetable oil
2 stalks scallions, finely chopped
1 Tbs ginger root, finely chopped

PROCEDURES:

1. Clean the shrimps and pat dry thoroughly with paper towels; then marinate with egg white, tapioca starch, salt, and wine for at least 20 minutes.

2. Combine the seasoning sauce ingredients and stir until salt is dissolved.

3. Fry the cashew nuts in 6 Tbs heated oil over low heat until light brown. Remove, drain, and set aside to cool.

TO COOK:

4. Heat the same oil used to fry the cashew nuts; drop in shrimps and stir-fry for 1 minute or until they change color. Remove shrimps and drain oil from wok.

5. Add another 2 Tbs of oil to wok; stir-fry the chopped scallion and ginger, then quickly add the shrimps and seasoning sauce. Stir over high heat until thoroughly mixed. Turn off heat, add cashew nuts and mix well. Serve hot.

NOTE: Shrimps taste best when served immediately after stir-frying. Since the final cooking time is very short, this dish is best when done as a last-minute, stir-fried dish.

Braised Soy Sauce Chicken　醬油鷄

This is an excellent dish for buffet dinners or large parties because it can be served either cold or at room temperature. Practically all my students love this beautiful dish, and "It tastes divine!" is the exclamation they use. The chicken has a rich brown color, and a sweet and winy flavor with a hint of star anise. The rock sugar not only thickens the sauce somewhat but also adds a glaze.

Leftover sauce can be kept refrigerated for several weeks. It can be used two or three times again to cook the same chicken dish. Just add ½ cup dark soy sauce, 2 Tbs wine, 1 star anise, 3 slices of ginger root, and rock sugar to taste to the leftover sauce and cook the chicken the same way. Although some Chinese call this master sauce "thousand-year-old sauce," it should not be kept too long because it will get moldy.

INGREDIENTS:
4 lb (2 kg) roasting chicken
1½ cup dark soy sauce
2 cups cold water
¼ cup Chinese rice wine
5 slices ginger root
1 whole star anise
½ cup rock sugar, broken into small pieces
1 Tbs sesame oil

PROCEDURES:

1. Wash the chicken inside and out under cold running water. Dry thoroughly with paper towels.

TO COOK:

2. In a heavy pot just large enough to hold the chicken snugly, bring the soy sauce, water, wine, ginger root, and star anise to a boil, then add the chicken. The liquid should reach halfway up the side of the chicken.

3. Bring to a boil again, reduce to moderate heat and cook, covered, for 20 minutes. Turn the chicken over, add the rock sugar and simmer 20 minutes longer, basting frequently. Turn off the heat, cover the pot and let the chicken cook for ½ hour to 1 hour.

4. Transfer the chicken to a chopping board and brush it with sesame oil.

TO CUT AND REASSEMBLE THE CHICKEN:

5. With a cleaver disjoin the wings and the leg with thigh on each side. Set aside. Now turn the body on its side, cut through it lengthwise so that the entire breast is separated from the back. Now the chicken is cut into 6 pieces (2 wings, 2 legs with thighs, and 1 back and 1 breast).

6. First chop the entire back piece crosswise into 1-inch-wide (2.5-cm) pieces. Arrange them in the center of a platter. Then cut the entire breast the same way into 1-inch-wide (2.5-cm) pieces. Place them on top of the back pieces.

7. Cut each wing at one joint into 2 pieces and place them at each side of the body. Finally chop the leg with thigh crosswise into 4 or 5 pieces and place them at their respective places around the body. (See the illustration for Odd-Flavor Chicken on page 110.)

8. Pour some sauce over the entire chicken and serve at room temperature.

Stir-Fried Lovers' Shrimp 鴛鴦蝦仁

This is an extremely beautiful and flattering dish to present. The shrimps are served half white and half seasoned with the reddish tomato catsup on either side of the crisp green fresh snow peas. The Chinese name for this dish is "Love Birds Shrimp" or "*Yuan Yang* Shrimp." *Yuan* and *Yang* are birds always seen lovingly together. Therefore they are often used as symbols of love and happiness. In China double pillows and bed covers embroidered with the *yuan* and *yang* birds are often given as wedding gifts.

Here the white shrimp represents the chastity, virtue, and beauty of the female bird; the red shrimp symbolizes the valor and courage of the male bird.

INGREDIENTS:
1 lb (500 g) frozen peeled and deveined shrimps
½ tsp salt
1 Tbs Chinese rice wine } to marinate shrimps
1 egg white
1 Tbs tapioca starch
½ lb (250 g) fresh snow peas or broccoli
½ tsp salt
1 Tbs wine } combined seasoning sauce
2 tsp sesame oil
9 Tbs peanut or vegetable oil
3 stalks scallions, cut into ¼-inch (6-mm) pieces
10 slices ginger
3 Tbs tomato catsup

PROCEDURES:
1. Defrost shrimps; rinse with cold water and pat dry thoroughly with paper towels. Marinate in the marinade ingredients.
2. Nip off the ends of the snow peas, then parboil and set aside.
3. Mix the combined sauce ingredients.

TO COOK:
4. Heat 1 Tbs oil in wok, stir-fry the snow peas for a few seconds, add a sprinkling of salt. Mix well; remove and place in the center of a serving platter.
5. Heat 8 Tbs oil in wok. Stir-fry the marinated shrimps for 15 to 20 seconds until the shrimps change color. Remove shrimps with a strainer; drain oil from wok.
6. Pour 1 Tbs of the used oil into wok. Sauté the scallions and ginger slices for a few seconds. Add shrimps and stir quickly. Pour in the combined seasoning sauce. Mix thoroughly and remove half of the shrimp and put them on one side of the platter.
7. Add 3 Tbs catsup to the shrimp in the wok and stir for a few seconds. Remove and put on the other side of the platter. Serve hot.

NOTE: This dish is best when served as a last-minute stir-frying dish.

Abalone in Oyster Sauce　燒油鮑脯

Abalone is considered a delicacy by the Orientals and is often used in banquet dishes. The meat is from a mollusk found in the Pacific Ocean, especially near Mexico and Japan. Smooth-textured and pleasant-tasting, abalone can be eaten directly from the can, sliced thin for a cold appetizer, shredded or sliced to be stir-fried with vegetables or meat, or cut into chunks to be simmered with meat or poultry.

This is an exquisite dish: tender white abalone slices on a bed of green Chinese cabbage covered with an oyster-flavored, shining brown sauce. It is definitely worth trying.

INGREDIENTS:

1 lb (500 g) Chinese cabbage
2 cups chicken broth
½ tsp salt
one 15-oz (500-g) can abalone
2 Tbs peanut or vegetable oil
1 Tbs Chinese rice wine
2 Tbs oyster sauce
1 Tbs dark soy sauce
1 tsp sugar
1 Tbs tapioca starch dissolved in 1 Tbs water
1 Tbs sesame oil

PROCEDURES:

1. Wash and then cut the Chinese cabbage into 2-inch (5-cm) pieces. Bring 1 cup chicken broth and ½ tsp salt to a boil. Drop in half of the cabbage and cook for about ½ minute. Drain and arrange cabbage on a serving plate. Add rest of cabbage to the same broth and repeat the procedure. Discard broth.

2. Cut abalone into round pieces ⅛ inch (3 mm) thick. Place in boiling water and boil for about 5 seconds. Remove and set aside.

TO COOK:

3. Heat 2 Tbs oil in wok, splash in wine, and add 1 cup chicken broth. Bring to a boil, then add oyster sauce, soy sauce, and sugar. When it boils again, add abalone and the tapioca starch paste, stirring constantly. When liquid thickens, garnish with sesame oil and attractively place the abalone over the cabbage. Pour the remaining sauce on top. Serve hot.

NOTE: The abalone packaged in a can is already cooked. Therefore the cooking should be limited to a few minutes, since prolonged cooking will toughen the abalone.

Shrimp in Lobster Sauce 蝦龍糊

This dish is so named not because it contains lobster meat but because the same sauce is used to cook lobster, as in Lobster Cantonese. It is a very popular dish in America, both because of its delicious white sauce and because of the succulent crispness of the shrimp. The fermented black beans also add a rich aroma and flavor to this dish.

Since this dish is saucy, it goes very well with rice.

INGREDIENTS:

1 lb (500 g) frozen peeled and deveined shrimps, uncooked
1 Tbs light soy sauce
1 Tbs Chinese rice wine ⎫
½ tsp salt   ⎬ to marinate shrimp
½ tsp sugar   ⎭
1 Tbs tapioca starch dissolved in 2 Tbs water
4 Tbs peanut or vegetable oil
2 cloves garlic, crushed
2 tsp salted black beans (fermented black beans), coarsely chopped
¼ lb (125 g) ground pork
2 stalks scallions, cut into 2-inch (5-cm) pieces
½ cup water or chicken broth
2 eggs, lightly beaten

PROCEDURES:

1. Thaw and then rinse shrimps in cold water. Pat completely dry with paper towels. Marinate with soy sauce, wine, salt, and sugar for 20 to 30 minutes. Dissolve tapioca starch in water.

TO COOK:

2. Heat 2 Tbs oil in a wok. Add the garlic and the black beans. Stir a few times. Then add the ground pork and continue stirring until the pork turns white. Remove and set aside.

3. Heat another 2 Tbs oil in wok. Add the scallions and shrimps. Stir until the shrimps change color. Mix in the ground pork with black beans; stir well. Add ½ cup water and bring to boil. Cover and cook over medium heat for 3 minutes. Thicken with the predissolved tapioca starch. Finally stir in the beaten eggs. Turn off the flame immediately and serve.

NOTE: Medium-size fresh shrimps can be used in place of the frozen peeled and deveined shrimps.

Spareribs with Fermented Black Beans 豆豉排骨

These spareribs are first seared in hot oil with garlic to acquire a protective shield, then steam-cooked vigorously with the fermented (salted) black beans, rice wine, and the marinade. The result is tender succulent spareribs, full of the rich flavors of the fermented black beans and garlic.

This dish is often served as one of the *dim sum* in tea houses. But it is also excellent when served as hors d'oeuvres or one of the main dishes.

INGREDIENTS:

2 lb (1 kg) rack of spareribs
4 Tbs dark soy sauce } to marinate spareribs
1 Tbs sugar
2 Tbs peanut or vegetable oil
2 cloves garlic, crushed
1½ Tbs salted black beans, coarsely chopped
2 Tbs Chinese rice wine
1 cup water
1 tsp tapioca starch dissolved in 1 Tbs water

PROCEDURES:

1. Trim the fat from spareribs. Chop the spareribs across the bones into 1½-inch-long (4-cm) sections with a cleaver; separate each rib. Marinate with soy sauce and sugar for about 20 minutes. Reserve the marinade.

TO COOK:

2. Heat a wok very hot. Add oil, then garlic and spareribs. Stir-fry until the spareribs are lightly browned on both sides (about 1 minute). Add the salted black beans, wine, the reserved marinade, and water. Bring to a boil, cover, reduce to low heat, and simmer for about 1 hour. Stir two or three times during cooking. Mix in the well-stirred tapioca starch. Stir until the sauce thickens. Serve hot.

NOTE: You can ask your butcher to cut the sparerib rack across the bones into 1½-inch-long (4-cm) strips. It is easier then for you to separate the ribs. This dish can be prepared and cooked totally ahead of time. Just remember not to thicken the sauce until you are ready to serve. The cooked spareribs can be left in the wok or a large pot. Just before serving, bring to a boil to thoroughly heat the spareribs, then thicken the sauce and serve.

Chinese Fried Noodles, Both Sides Brown 兩面黃炒麵

Since the staple food of northern China is wheat, northerners usually eat noodles, buns, dumplings, pancakes, and so on, for their supply of carbohydrates. To the rest of the country, wheat products are primarily snacks, called *dim sum*. But noodles, which symbolize longevity, are frequently served as a main dish at birthdays all over China. The Chinese enjoy swishing and tossing the noodles in the broth or sauce before sucking them up, and they don't mind making noises when they eat noodles, especially noodles in soup.

Both-sides-brown fried noodles is the fanciest way to serve noodles and this dish is considered a treat. The boiled noodles are first shallow-fried until crunchy and golden brown on both sides, then crowned with a glazed topping of stir-fried meat and vegetables. The noodles acquire flavors from the thickened sauce, but they are not soaked through. The Canton noodles, made of alimentary paste, are the best for this type of cooking since they are crispy and fine.

INGREDIENTS:
½ lb (250 g) dried Canton noodles
9 Tbs peanut or vegetable oil
1 cup raw pork or beef, shredded to 2-inch (5-cm) strips
1 Tbs light soy sauce ⎫
1 tsp Chinese rice wine ⎬ to marinate shredded pork
½ Tbs tapioca starch ⎭
6 to 8 Chinese dried mushrooms
2 Tbs tapioca starch
1½ cups chicken broth
3 cups Chinese cabbage, shredded
1 cup bamboo shoots, shredded
1 tsp salt

PROCEDURES:
1. Place the dried Canton noodles in boiling water for about 1 minute. Then take out immediately and rinse with cold water and drain. Mix the noodles with 2 Tbs oil to prevent sticking and set aside.
2. Marinate meat with soy sauce, wine, and tapioca starch.
3. Soak the dried mushrooms in hot water until soft. Remove and discard the stems. Shred the mushrooms. Set aside.
4. Mix the 2 Tbs tapioca starch with ½ cup chicken broth.

TO COOK:
5. Heat 5 Tbs oil in a wok. Add noodles; fry over medium high heat until the bottom is golden brown, then turn over to brown the other side. Keep the browned noodle cake in a warm oven while cooking the sauce.
6. Heat 2 Tbs oil in the wok; stir in the meat mixture and stir-fry for about 2 minutes. Add the shredded cabbage, mushrooms, bamboo shoots, salt, and remaining 1 cup of chicken broth. Cook over medium high heat until tender, stir-

ring constantly. Mix in the tapioca starch mixture. When liquid has thickened, pour over the noodle cake and serve immediately.

NOTE: Both sides of the noodles can be browned ahead of time and kept at room temperature. Just before serving, preheat the oven to 375° F (182° C) and warm up the fried noodles in the oven while doing the sauce in the wok. Chicken or shrimp can be used instead of pork or beef.

Fried Chicken Slices with Lemon Sauce 檸檬鷄片

This is a favorite dish for family meals, for entertaining, and even for banquets. Light and gleaming, the crunchy chicken slices are full of lingering good tastes. The final touch of the combined sauce adds taste and aroma to the chicken without making it sour. This dish goes well with rice and a colorful, stir-fried vegetable dish. Water chestnut flour is used to make the crust extremely light and crunchy.

INGREDIENTS:

2 whole skinned and boned chicken breasts or chicken cutlets, uncooked

1 egg yolk
1 tsp salt
1 Tbs Chinese rice wine
1 Tbs light soy sauce
¼ tsp white pepper
1 Tbs tapioca starch dissolved in 1 Tbs water
} to marinate chicken

6 Tbs fresh lemon juice
6 Tbs sugar
6 Tbs chicken broth
1 tsp salt
1 Tbs tapioca starch
2 tsp sesame oil
} combined seasoning sauce

6 Tbs tapioca starch
3 Tbs water chestnut flour
} to coat chicken before frying

2 cups peanut or vegetable oil
some Chinese parsley
6 lemon slices
} to garnish

PROCEDURES:

1. Cut chicken into thin slices 1½ inches (4 cm) wide and 2 inches (5 cm) long. Marinate with the ingredients listed above.

2. Mix the combined seasoning sauce in a bowl.

3. Mix the 6 Tbs tapioca starch and 3 Tbs water chestnut flour on a plate.

TO COOK:

4. Coat each piece of chicken with the starch and flour mixture and deep-fry the chicken slices over low heat for about 2 minutes until golden brown. Remove with a wired strainer.

5. Heat the oil very hot. Deep-fry the chicken again for another 10 to 20 seconds. Drain and place on a plate.

6. Heat another 1 Tbs oil. Stir-fry the combined seasoning sauce; when it boils and thickens, pour the sauce onto the fried chicken slices. Garnish with the Chinese parsley leaves and lemon slices. Serve hot.

NOTE: This dish can be cooked ahead of time up through step 4. Just before serving, follow the rest of the instructions.

Chinese Fire Pot with Assorted Meats and Vegetables 六生火鍋

The fire pot offers a simple but enjoyable way to eat. There is no cooking art involved, but the flavor is exotic and savory, and the beautiful display of thinly cut ingredients will impress your guests.

Originating with the Mongols as a way of keeping food hot throughout the meal, the fire pot, or *huo guo*, has gone through much refinement over the centuries. The cooking pot itself underwent a transformation from a pot over a brazier to a beautiful and ingenious utensil made of brass, copper, aluminum, or stainless steel, with a compartment for charcoal or sterno. Electric fire pots are available now to make the cooking easier and more practical.

The meal begins when the fire pot containing boiling broth is placed in the center of the table. Platters of thinly cut raw meats, poultry, seafood, mushrooms, and other vegetables are placed around the pot. Small serving cups containing different sauce dips are also placed on the table. Each diner is provided with a rice bowl and a pair of chopsticks and makes his or her own sauce dip in the bowl. Small brass strainers are now available for those who cannot use chopsticks. The guests take whatever ingredient they like and dip it into the boiling broth. In less than half a minute the food is cooked. It is then dipped into the combined sauce and eaten. At the end of the meal, some noodles can be cooked in the tasty broth.

INGREDIENTS:
1 lb (500 g) fresh shrimps
1 lb (500 g) London broil or other thick steak
1 whole boned and skinned chicken breast or chicken cutlet
10 to 16 dried Chinese mushrooms
¼ lb (125 g) bean thread
3 cakes bean curd
½ lb (250 g) Chinese cabbage
3 cups chicken broth
10 eggs
light soy sauce
Chinese Chin Kiang vinegar
fermented bean curd (fu ju), *mashed*   } *sauce dips (place each sauce in a*
barbecue sauce (sha cha *sauce*)   *separate small serving bowl)*
chili paste with garlic
hoisin sauce
oyster sauce

PROCEDURES:
1. Shell and devein the shrimps. Rinse with cold water. Cut each horizontally into two thin slices. Arrange nicely on a plate.

2. Cut the beef and chicken into thin slices. Arrange on separate plates.

3. Soak the Chinese mushrooms in hot water for about 15 minutes. Cut off and discard the stems. Cut large ones in half.

4. Soak the bean thread in hot water for about 10 minutes. Then cut into 3-inch-long sections.

5. Cut the bean curd and Chinese cabbage into inch-long pieces.

6. In a large pot, boil the chicken broth and the liquid used to soak the mushrooms. When the broth boils, pour it into the fire pot.

7. Ask each individual to beat an egg in his or her own rice bowl. Then scoop in a little (about 1 tsp) sauce from each serving cup and beat together with the egg to make the sauce dip.

TO COOK:

8. With chopsticks take whatever ingredient you want from the platter and swish it in the boiling broth. When the food is cooked (less than ½ minute usually), take it out and dip it into the sauce and eat.

NOTE: Canned abalone, clams, fillet of fish, and lamb can be added.

Chicken with Walnuts 核桃鶏丁

This is a lovely and delicate dish—succulent white diced chicken mixed with crisp green peppers and garnished with crunchy, light brown walnuts. It is a triumph of natural colors and flavors. It is worth the effort to remove the dark skin from the walnuts, because the skin is rather tart. In restaurants this dish is made brown with the addition of sweet bean sauce (see note below).

By the way, the Chinese believe that walnuts are good for the hair. Postnatal care for the mother often includes eating walnuts to combat the losing of hair.

INGREDIENTS:
2 whole chicken breasts or chicken cutlets
1 egg white
1 tsp salt
1 Tbs Chinese rice wine } *to marinate chicken*
2 tsp tapioca starch
¾ cup shelled walnuts
¾ cup green pepper, cut into 1-inch (2.5-cm) squares
1 cup peanut or vegetable oil
1 tsp sugar
1 tsp salt
1 tsp tapioca starch dissolved in 2 Tbs water

PROCEDURES:
1. Cut the chicken into ½-inch (1.5-cm) cubes. Marinate with the egg white, salt, wine, and tapioca starch for at least 30 minutes.
2. Put walnuts in 2 cups boiling water. Boil for 1 minute, then remove a few at a time and peel off the skins. Set aside.
3. Parboil green pepper for 1 minute. Rinse in cold water and drain well.
4. Heat 1 cup oil in a wok and fry the peeled walnuts for about 2 minutes or until lightly browned. Do not allow them to get too dark, for walnuts burn quickly. Remove and drain on paper towels.

TO COOK:
5. Pour off (but reserve) all but 4 Tbs oil. Heat the oil over moderate heat and stir-fry the chicken until most of the chicken changes color. Add sugar and salt and the cooked green pepper; mix well.
6. Stir the tapioca starch and water well and pour over the chicken. Stir until the sauce thickens and coats the chicken with a clear glaze. Remove to a platter and garnish with the walnuts. Serve hot.

NOTE: Two Tbs of sweet bean sauce can be used instead of 1 tsp salt and 1 tsp sugar in step 5. This will add a rich brown color and mellow taste to the dish.

Stuffed Bean Curd, Cantonese Style 釀豆腐

This is a fancy way of eating the nutritious bean curd (*to fu*). It is a delicate, dainty, and palatable dish, beautifully garnished with the glazy brown sauce and shredded green scallions. Dried shrimps are highly valued by the Chinese as a seasoning. If you do not like the "fishy" smell of the dried shrimps, soak them overnight with rice wine before chopping and mixing them with the meat.

INGREDIENTS:
4 cakes firm Chinese bean curd
¼ lb (125 g) ground pork
1 Tbs dried shrimps
1 Tbs light soy sauce
1 Tbs Chinese rice wine ⎱
¼ tsp salt ⎰ to marinate ground pork
½ Tbs tapioca starch
1 stalk scallion, chopped
⅓ cup peanut or vegetable oil
1 cup chicken broth
1 Tbs dark soy sauce
1 Tbs oyster sauce
1 Tbs tapioca starch dissolved in 1 Tbs cold water
2 stalks scallions, shredded

PROCEDURES:
1. Press the bean curd with a heavy weight or with 2 or 3 chopping boards for about ½ hour to reduce excess water. Then cut each piece diagonally into 4 triangular pieces.

2. Soak the dried shrimps in hot water for 20 to 30 minutes and chop them fine.

3. Marinate the ground pork with the soy sauce, wine, salt, and tapioca starch for at least 15 minutes; mix in the chopped dried shrimps and chopped scallion.

4. Cut a slit on the long side of each bean curd triangle. Take out some bean curd and stuff the opening carefully with the meat mixture.

TO COOK:
5. Heat the oil in a wok. Arrange the bean curd, meat side down, in the wok and fry for 2 minutes until brown. Add 1 cup chicken broth, cover and simmer for 3 to 4 minutes. Dish the bean curd out carefully onto a plate and arrange them attractively lying down.

6. Add dark soy sauce and oyster sauce to the liquid in the wok. Bring to a boil and thicken with tapioca starch mixture. Pour this sauce on top of the bean curd and garnish with shredded scallion.

NOTE: The stuffed bean curd can be browned and simmered ahead of time as in step 5. Just before serving heat the stuffed bean curd with its liquid in a wok or saucepan. Place the bean curd pieces on a plate and then follow step 6 to finish the dish.

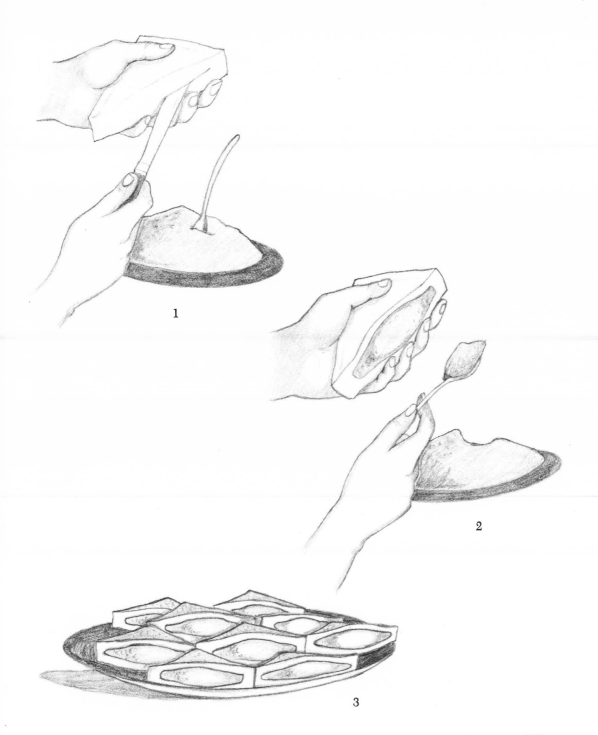

Deep-Fried Cellophane Noodles and Minced Chicken Wrapped in Lettuce Leaves 生炒鷄鬆

This dish is fun to serve and is extremely well liked by everybody who has tasted it in the cooking school. It is easy to understand why: the crunchy white cellophane noodles are mixed with the colorful and tasty diced ham, chicken, mushrooms, bamboo shoots, peas, and egg and wrapped with the crispy lettuce leaves. The delicious flavor coupled with the crunchy noise when eating is what makes this dish special.

INGREDIENTS:

1 skinned and boned whole chicken breast or chicken cutlet
½ tsp salt
1 Tbs Chinese rice wine } *to marinate chicken*
1 Tbs tapioca starch
6 to 8 dried mushrooms
½ cup green peas
2 eggs
1½ Tbs light soy sauce
½ tsp salt
1 tsp sesame oil } *combined seasoning sauce*
⅛ tsp white or black pepper
2 Tbs chicken broth
2 oz (60 g) cellophane noodles
1 cup peanut or vegetable oil
¼ cup Smithfield ham
1 cup bamboo shoots, diced
20 lettuce leaves (nice round pieces)

PROCEDURES:

1. Dice the chicken into ¼-inch (6-mm) cubes. Marinate with salt, wine, and tapioca starch for at least 20 minutes.

2. Boil Smithfield ham for 10 minutes. When cool, dice the ham into ¼-inch (6-mm) cubes.

3. Soak mushrooms in hot water until soft. Remove and discard stems and dice mushrooms same size as other ingredients. Parboil green peas for about 1 minute. Rinse with cold water.

4. Beat the eggs. Make several pancakes in the wok. (Please see Agar-Agar Salad with Ham on page 22 for the instructions on how to make the egg pancakes.) When cool, cut into ¼-inch (6-mm) pieces.

5. Combine the sauce ingredients.

6. Cut and loosen the cellophane noodles and separate them into several batches. Heat 1 cup oil until very hot. Deep-fry the cellophane noodles, a few at a time, until puffed up (only 2 or 3 seconds on each side). Place on a platter.

7. Heat 2 Tbs oil in wok. Stir-fry the marinated diced chicken for about ½ minute or until it turns white. Drain and set aside.

8. Heat 2 Tbs oil in wok. Stir-fry the diced ham, mushrooms, bamboo shoots, and green peas for about 1 minute. Add the cooked chicken, diced egg, and combined seasoning sauce. Stir over high heat until mixed thoroughly. Remove and put on the platter over the cellophane noodles.

9. Each diner should help himself or herself by putting some of the meat and noodle mixture in one lettuce leaf, wrapping the leaf around the mixture, and eating it.

NOTE: The cellophane noodles can be deep-fried ahead of time and kept in a tightly covered jar or container. The meat and vegetables can be stir-fried and kept warm in the oven. Do not combine the two until you are ready to serve.

Shark's Fin Soup 魚翅湯

Shark's fin is one of the most elegant and expensive foods in China. Many Chinese have never tasted shark's fin in their lives. It is actually the dried cartilage taken from fins of a particular species of sharks. The process used to remove the fishy odor is long and laborious, involving many days of soaking, simmering, cleaning, and finally cooking over low heat. Fortunately, shark's fins are now available in cans, skinned and cleaned. They are also available in dried form, which must be soaked before using. Now Americans can serve this banquet dish formerly eaten only by the Chinese gourmets.

INGREDIENTS:
1 whole chicken cutlet or breast, skinned and boned
½ egg white ⎫
½ tsp salt ⎪
1 tsp Chinese rice wine ⎬ *to marinate chicken*
1 tsp tapioca starch ⎭
4 to 6 dried mushrooms
one 10-oz (about 250-g) can shark's fin soup
3 cups chicken broth
1 cup water
1 Tbs ginger root, shredded
1 Tbs Chinese rice wine
⅛ tsp white pepper
1 Tbs light soy sauce
2 Tbs tapioca starch dissolved in ¼ cup water
½ lb (250 g) Smithfield ham

PROCEDURES:
1. Cook Smithfield ham in boiling water for about 10 to 15 minutes. Cool, then shred into 1½-inch-long (4-cm) julienne strips.
2. Cut the chicken cutlet into ⅛-inch-thick (3-mm) slices; cut again into 1½-inch-long (4-cm) julienne strips. Marinate with egg white, salt, wine, and tapioca starch for at least 20 minutes.
3. Soak dried mushrooms in hot water for about 20 minutes. Remove and discard stems. Cut into julienne strips.
4. Remove the shark's fin pieces from the can. Separate or shred the large pieces. Then put the long shredded strips with the broth from the can into a large bowl.

TO COOK:

5. Bring the 3 cups of chicken broth, 1 cup water, and the shark's fin soup to a boil. Add ginger, wine, and white pepper and simmer for 5 minutes. Add shredded mushrooms, light soy sauce, and then the chicken. Stir to separate the shreds. Remove the scum that accumulates on top. Mix the tapioca starch well and slowly pour it in; stir until the soup thickens and boils again. Garnish with the shredded ham and serve hot.

NOTE: This soup can be cooked ahead of time, but do not thicken or garnish it until you are ready to serve. Shredded bamboo shoots can be added if desired.

Assorted Delicacies Soup in Winter Melon 竹錦冬瓜盅

As mentioned before, soup is very important in China. It is considered a beverage and is served throughout the meal. Tea is served before or after meals. At banquets in China, two or three soups are served between courses to whet and rekindle the appetite. In some areas, a large bowl of soup is placed at the center of the table at the start of a meal because the diners are often thirsty then. At the end of the meal, the soup is reheated and served again to wash down all the food.

This delicate, tasty soup served in the winter melon is truly impressive. Though time-consuming, most of the preparation can be done one day in advance.

INGREDIENTS:
1 whole skinned and boned chicken breast or chicken cutlet
2 dried scallops or 2 Tbs dried shrimps
4 to 6 dried mushrooms
7 to 8 lb (4 kg) winter melon (use 7 or 8 inches of the part without stem)
¼ lb (125 g) cooked Smithfield ham, diced small
¼ lb (125 g) peeled and deveined raw shrimps
10 straw mushrooms
½ cup bamboo shoots, diced
6 to 8 fresh water chestnuts, peeled and diced
½ cup green peas
5 cups chicken broth
1 Tbs ginger root, chopped
1 tsp salt
1 Tbs Chinese rice wine

PROCEDURES:
1. Cook the chicken cutlet in boiling water for about 15 minutes. Dice into small cubes.

2. Soak dried scallops in hot water for about 20 minutes. Steam for about ½ hour until soft. When cool, tear into fine shreds.

3. Soak the dried mushrooms in hot water until soft. Remove the stems and cut into small pieces.

4. Wash the skin of the winter melon. Remove the top of the melon by cutting horizontally about 2 inches (5 cm) from the stem so that a 7- or 8-inch (17.5-cm or 20-cm) high melon bowl is left. Remove the seeds. Make the inside area of the melon larger by cutting about ½ to 1 inch (1.5 to 2.5 cm) of the pulp from the melon. Dice the white pulp into ¼-inch (6-mm) cubes to be included in the soup.

5. Carve the rim of melon into a zigzag pattern. If desired, carve a design on the outer skin as well. Place the melon in a soup bowl and steam for ½ hour or until soft.

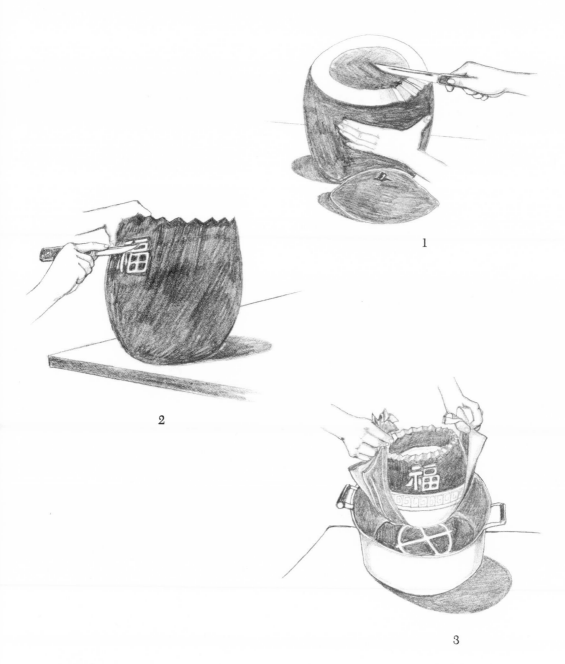

1

2

3

TO COOK:

6. Put the chicken, ham, shrimps, mushrooms, straw mushrooms, bamboo shoots, water chestnuts, diced winter melon, green peas, and scallops with liquid in a big pot. Add 5 cups chicken broth and bring to a boil. Season with ginger, salt, and wine. Continue to cook for 10 minutes.

7. Pour the soup into the winter melon. With the melon in a large soup bowl, steam about 15 minutes. Serve soup hot in the melon.

NOTE: All but steps 5 and 7 can be done a day in advance.

Buddha's Delight 羅漢齋

Buddha's Delight is a favorite vegetarian dish in China and is considered a ban-quet-style dish for the Buddhists. Usually more than 10 ingredients are used in this dish, and every region has its own version. The final touch of the fermented bean curd adds a zest to the ingredients.

This dish typifies the stir-fry method for Chinese vegetables. The ingredients are first seared briefly in hot oil, then steam-cooked in soy sauce and mushroom water. The result is plump, crisp vegetables with vivid coloring and exotic taste. No wonder it is called Buddha's Delight.

INGREDIENTS:

4 dried Chinese mushrooms
10 baby corn
½ lb (250 g) Chinese cabbage,
    cut to 1- by 2-inch (2.5- by
    5-cm) pieces
½ cup carrots, sliced
¼ cup bamboo shoots, sliced
¼ cup lotus root, sliced
} group A ingredients

30 canned gingko nuts
2 oz (60 g) cellophane noodles
2 Tbs tree ears
16 golden needles
2 oz (60 g) dried bean curd slices
½ cup five-spiced brown bean curd,
    sliced ⅛ inch (3 mm) thick
} group B ingredients

6 fresh water chestnuts
½ lb (250 g) fresh snow peas
5 Tbs peanut or vegetable oil
1½ tsp salt
2 tsp sugar
2½ Tbs light soy sauce
2 Tbs fermented bean curd
1 Tbs sesame oil

PROCEDURES:

1. Soak the dried mushrooms, tree ears, golden needles, cellophane noodles, and dried bean curd slices in hot water in separate bowls for 20 to 30 minutes until soft. Cut off and discard mushroom stems, then cut each mushroom in half, reserving the mushroom water for later use. Cut the soaked cellophane noodles into 4-inch (10-cm) lengths; cut the dried bean curd into 1- by 2-inch (2.5- by 5-cm) pieces.

2. Set the baby corn, Chinese cabbage, carrots, bamboo shoots, and lotus root on a large plate with the mushrooms. These are group A ingredients.

3. Boil the gingko nuts in salted water for 5 minutes. Drain and set aside with the cellophane noodles, tree ears, golden needles, dried bean curd slices, and five-spiced brown bean curd. These are group B ingredients.

4. Peel and slice fresh water chestnuts. String and parboil the snow peas. Set aside with water chestnuts.

TO COOK:

5. Heat 3 Tbs oil in wok over medium-high heat and stir-fry group A ingredients for 2 to 3 minutes. Remove and set aside.

6. Heat 2 Tbs oil in wok over medium heat. Stir-fry group B ingredients for 1 minute. Add the cooked group A ingredients. Stir and mix well. Add salt, sugar, light soy sauce, and also the reserved mushroom water together with enough water to make 1½ cups. Mix well. Cover and cook for 10 minutes over medium-low heat.

7. Add the water chestnut slices, the snow peas, the fermented bean curd, and sesame oil; stir and mix well. Serve hot.

NOTE: To make this dish easier for cooking, the ingredients can be divided into three groups. On platter A put all the vegetables (baby corn, cabbage, carrots, bamboo shoots, and lotus roots) and the mushrooms; on platter B put the gingko nuts, cellophane noodles, tree ears, golden needles, dried bean curd slices, and five-spiced brown bean curd. The water chestnuts and parboiled snow peas can be set on another plate and put in at the last minute.

Princess Chicken 龍芽鳳翼

This is definitely a banquet-style dish because only the best ingredients are used. The center section of the chicken wing, considered a delicacy by the Chinese, is stuffed with shredded mushrooms, ham, and bamboo shoots. These delicious and delicate wings can be served either as hors d'oeuvres or a main dish. When served as hors d'oeuvres, the vegetables (mushrooms, bamboo shoot slices, and snow peas) can be omitted.

INGREDIENTS:
12 strips dried mushrooms
12 large chicken wings
12 strips cooked Smithfield ham, 2 by ¼ by ¼ inch
  (5-cm by 6-mm by 6-mm strips)
12 strips bamboo shoots, 2 by ¼ by ¼ inches (5-cm by 6-mm by 6-mm strips)
½ tsp salt
1 Tbs light soy sauce } *to marinate stuffed wings*
1 Tbs Chinese rice wine
1 Tbs oyster sauce
2 tsp light soy sauce
2 Tbs cold water } *combined seasoning sauce*
1 tsp tapioca starch
½ tsp sugar
4 to 6 dried mushrooms
2 Tbs peanut or vegetable oil
2 slices ginger
2 stalks scallions, cut into 2-inch (5-cm) lengths
½ cup bamboo shoots, cut into thin slices
¼ lb (125 g) snow peas, or ¼ cup green pepper, cut into 1-inch (2.5-cm) squares
½ cup reserved broth

PROCEDURES:
   1. Soak the dried mushrooms; then cut into strips 2 by ¼ by ¼ inch (5 cm by 6 mm by 6 mm). Boil Smithfield ham for 10 minutes; then cut into 2- by ¼ - by ¼ -inch (5- by 6- by 6-mm) strips. Cut bamboo shoots into 12 strips of the same size as the others.
   2. Wash the chicken wings. Cut off the wing tips and third sections (reserve for other uses). Only the center portions of the wings are used in this dish. To bone the center section, chop off a small piece of bone at each end with a cleaver and drop all the wings in 2 cups of boiling water. Boil for 3 to 4 minutes, and then remove from the pan and cool until touchable. Save the broth for later use. Sever the tendons at both ends of each piece and gently push the bones out with your fingers. Immediately place 1 strip each of mushroom, ham, and bamboo shoot in the cavity left by removing the bones. Repeat with all the wings.

3. Marinate the stuffed wings in salt, soy sauce, and wine for 20 to 30 minutes.

4. Combine the sauce ingredients and set aside.

5. Soak the dried mushrooms until soft and then cut into quarters.

TO COOK:

6. Heat a wok over high heat. Add the oil and stir-fry the ginger and scallion for a few seconds, then add the wings and brown them for 2 to 3 minutes; turn them over gently and cook for another minute. Add the mushrooms, bamboo shoot slices, and snow peas; then add ½ cup of reserved broth and cook for 2 minutes.

7. Mix the sauce ingredients thoroughly and pour into the wok; stir until the sauce thickens and coats the wings with a clear glaze. Serve hot.

NOTE: The chicken wings can be stuffed in advance and kept in the refrigerator. The mushrooms, bamboo shoots, and snow peas can be sliced before cooking. Then the final cooking time will be very short.

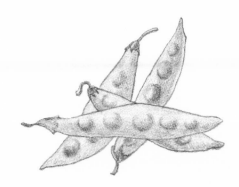

PART V

Hors D'Oeuvres

Shrimp Toasts 蝦仁吐司

See page 71 for this recipe.

Chinese Mushrooms Stuffed with Pork and Water Chestnuts

冬菇釀肉

This dish is truly a delicacy and can be served either as a main dish or as hors d'oeuvres. It is often served in the tea houses in China as *dim sum*. The chopped fresh water chestnuts add a crunchiness which contrasts nicely with the soft but tasty mushrooms. In addition, the glazed thick brown sauce that covers the stuffed mushrooms makes this dish extremely appetizing.

INGREDIENTS:
40 dried Chinese mushrooms, 1 to 1½ inches (2.5 cm to 4 cm) in diameter
6 to 10 fresh water chestnuts
½ lb (250 g) ground pork
1 Tbs dark soy sauce
1 Tbs Chinese rice wine } *filling*
½ tsp sugar
1 tsp tapioca starch
4 Tbs tapioca starch (to sprinkle on mushroom stems)
40 small leaves of Chinese parsley
2 Tbs peanut or vegetable oil
5 Tbs oyster sauce

PROCEDURES:
1. Soak the mushrooms in hot water for 20 minutes. Cut off and discard the stems. Strain the mushroom water and save ¾ cup of it.

2. Peel and then finely chop the water chestnuts. Mix the water chestnuts and ground pork with the soy sauce, wine, sugar, and 1 tsp tapioca starch. Mix them thoroughly.

3. Sprinkle a little tapioca starch on the stem sides of the mushrooms; then fill them with the pork mixture, smoothing it flat with a knife or your finger. Place a parsley leaf on top of each filled mushroom.

TO COOK:
4. Heat 2 Tbs oil in a wok over high heat; arrange the mushrooms side by side, stuffing side up, in a single layer in the wok. Reduce to moderate heat and brown the mushrooms lightly. Pour ¾ cup of the reserved mushroom water in the wok, add 5 Tbs oyster sauce, bring to a boil and cover the wok. Reduce to low heat and simmer for 20 minutes. Baste frequently; then transfer the mushrooms to a serving platter and pour the gravy over the mushrooms. Serve hot.

NOTE: The mushrooms can be stuffed and frozen for future use. This dish can also be prepared and cooked totally ahead of time. Heat by pouring ¼ cup mushroom water and 1 Tbs oyster sauce in the wok and simmering for about 5 minutes.

Deep-Fried Shrimp Balls 炸蝦球

See page 43 for this recipe.

Peking Dumplings with Pork and Vegetables (Shui Jiao) 水餃

In northern China, *shui jiao* is served as a main course and is considered a delicacy. When families, relatives, or close friends gather, *shui jiao* is often the most popular dish to serve because everybody can pitch in to help make the beautiful dumplings. The Chinese find it very relaxing to chat and work at the same time. Since *shui jiao* is shaped like an ingot, which was used as money until the beginning of the 20th century, it is one of the foods that must be served for the New Year to symbolize wealth. Since every family was chopping meat and cabbage to make *shui jiao* during the New Year season in Peking, the chopping sound could be heard throughout the whole city. (By the way, the Chinese believe that cleaver-chopped meat tastes better than machine-chopped meat.) Often a great quantity of *shui jiao* was made and stored in a big crock. The crock was usually placed outside in the yard and was not unlike a natural freezer during the winter months. People also exchanged gifts with the dumplings they made to wish each other good luck and good fortune.

INGREDIENTS:
1 pack shui jiao *wrappers (about 50 to 60 pieces)*
¾ lb (375 g) Chinese cabbage
1 lb (500 g) ground pork
2 stalks scallions, chopped
1 Tbs ginger, chopped fine
3 Tbs dark soy sauce } *filling*
1 Tbs Chinese rice wine
1 tsp salt
2 Tbs sesame oil
2 Tbs chicken broth
For dip, mix some soy sauce, Chin Kiang vinegar, and chili oil or mashed garlic in a small saucer

PROCEDURES:
   1. Thaw the *shui jiao* wrappers. Then open the package and cover the wrappers with wet towels for about 15 minutes before use.
   2. Wash the Chinese cabbage; chop it into fine pieces. Sprinkle a little salt on the chopped cabbage, wait a few minutes, then squeeze dry.
   3. Mix the ground pork, scallions, ginger, soy sauce, wine, salt, sesame oil, and chicken broth in a bowl thoroughly, then add the chopped cabbage. Mix to make the filling.

4. Place about 1 Tbs filling in center of *shui jiao* wrapper. Put some water around the edge and fold and pleat to make a dumpling. Press with finger again to make sure it is tightly sealed.

TO COOK:

5. Boil about 8 cups of water in a deep pot. Drop dumplings one by one into the boiling water. Stir to make sure they do not stick to the bottom. Cook for about ½ minute or until the water boils again. Add ⅔ cup cold water to the pot, cover, and let it come to a boil again. Then add another ⅔ cup cold water; when it boils again, add ⅔ cup of cold water for the third time. When the water boils again, the dumplings are ready. Remove the dumplings with the wired sieve to a plate.

6. Serve with dip.

NOTE: The dumplings can be made ahead of time and frozen before cooking. No need to defrost before cooking. They can be served as hors d'oeuvres or a main dish.

Shanghai Spring Rolls 上海春捲

Since the Chinese New Year often occurs in late January or February when spring is about to begin, spring rolls (called egg rolls here by Americans) are often served to symbolize the *rolling* in of *spring*. Furthermore, since the fried spring rolls resemble gold bars, which were once used as money in China, it is imperative that spring rolls be served at New Year dinners or parties. Businessmen often eat spring rolls before they go on a business trip. The traditional spring rolls are long and lean and are much more delicate than the "egg rolls" served in restaurants or available in supermarkets.

Spring rolls are excellent hors d'oeuvres and become one of the most popular dishes served at buffet dinners.

INGREDIENTS:

½ lb (250 g) lean pork or 2 pork chops
1 Tbs dark soy sauce ⎫
½ Tbs Chinese rice wine ⎬ to marinate shredded pork
1 tsp tapioca starch ⎭
8 to 10 Chinese dried mushrooms
½ lb (250 g) Chinese cabbage
½ lb (250 g) bean sprouts
4 cups peanut or vegetable oil
1½ Tbs dark soy sauce
½ tsp salt
½ cup chicken broth
1½ Tbs tapioca starch dissolved in 2 Tbs water
25 spring roll wrappers
4 Tbs flour mixed with 6 Tbs water (paste to seal wrappers)
2 Tbs thin soy sauce ⎫
1 Tbs Chin Kiang vinegar ⎬ dip (optional)

PROCEDURES:

1. Slice and then shred the pork; then marinate with 1 Tbs soy sauce, ½ Tbs wine, and 1 tsp tapioca starch.

2. Soak the Chinese mushrooms in hot water for about 15 minutes; then discard the stems and shred.

3. Rinse the Chinese cabbage and then shred. Rinse the bean sprouts with cold water, then drain.

4. Heat 2 Tbs oil in wok; stir-fry the marinated shredded pork for about ½ minute, drain and remove to a plate. Add the shredded cabbage to the wok, stir-fry for a moment, add the shredded mushrooms, soy sauce, salt, and chicken broth, cover and cook about 2 minutes. Then add pork and bean sprouts and stir-fry for about ½ minute over high heat. Thicken with tapioca paste and remove with a wired strainer to *cool* on a plate.

5. Place about 2 Tbs of the filling on each spring roll skin, roll tightly several

times, fold right side to center, then left side to center; put some flour paste on the outer edge of skin to seal and roll into a tight roll.

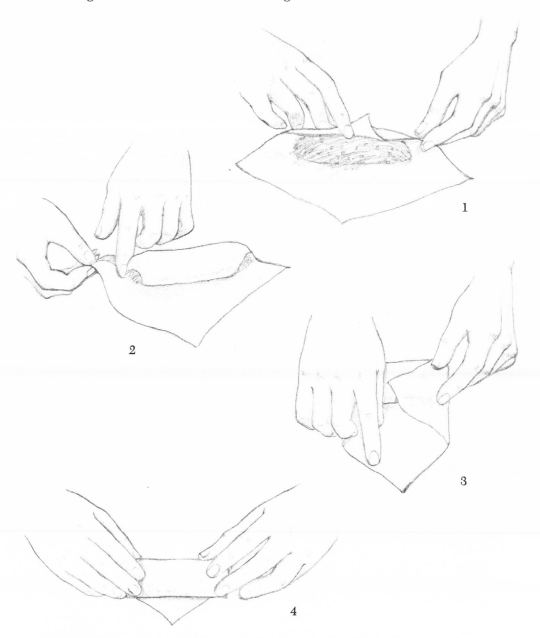

TO COOK:

6. Heat about 3½ cups of oil in wok over high heat; turn to medium heat, then deep-fry spring rolls until golden brown. Serve hot with dip.

NOTE: It is important to wait until the filling is cool before you stuff and make the spring rolls. Do not use too much sauce, either; otherwise the wrappers will be soaked through and break. The spring rolls can be made and deep-fried and frozen. Before serving, preheat the oven to 350° F (177° C) and bake for 15 to 20 minutes.

Steamed Pearl Balls 珍珠肉丸

See page 92 for this recipe.

Steamed Shao Mai (Dim Sum) 烧賣

These open-faced dumplings are delectable appetizers or hors d'oeuvres. They are one of the most popular *dim sum* served in tea houses in China. *"Dim Sum"* literally means "dot and heart," which is a general term and includes all sorts of dumplings, pastries, and noodle and rice dishes that are "to your heart's delight." Most of the *dim sum* can be served as snacks or lunches, for example, *shao mai*, wontons, *shui jiao,* fried dumplings, shrimp dumplings, and Chinese fried noodle both sides brown. They are also excellent breakfast items.

INGREDIENTS:
1 tsp salt
1½ cups Chinese cabbage, finely chopped
1 tsp salt
6 dried mushrooms
6 to 8 fresh water chestnuts
¼ lb (125 g) raw shrimps, peeled and deveined
1 lb (500 g) ground pork
2 Tbs light soy sauce } filling
1 Tbs Chinese rice wine
½ tsp sugar
1 Tbs tapioca starch
2 Tbs sesame oil
2 Tbs chicken broth
1 stalk scallion, finely chopped
1 Tbs ginger root, finely chopped
1 package shui jiao *wrappers*

PROCEDURES:
1. Put the chopped cabbage in a mixing bowl and sprinkle with 1 tsp salt. Mix well and let stand for 10 minutes. Then squeeze the excess water from the cabbage with both hands. Set aside.
2. Soak the dried mushrooms in hot water until soft (about 15 minutes). Cut off and discard stems. Dice and then chop the mushrooms. Peel and then chop the fresh water chestnuts. Dice the shrimps into ¼-inch (6-mm) pieces.
3. Combine the ground pork, shrimps, water chestnuts, and mushrooms with 1 tsp salt, soy sauce, wine, sugar, tapioca starch, sesame oil, chicken broth, scallion and ginger. Mix well; then add the cabbage and mix some more.
4. Cover the wrappers with a damp cloth to prevent them from drying out. To make *shao mai*, place about 1 Tbs filling in the center of each wrapper and moisten the side with a little water. Gather the sides of the wrapper around the

filling, letting the wrapper form small pleats naturally. Squeeze the middle gently to make sure the wrapper sticks firmly against the filling and press down on a flat surface so that the *shao mai* flattens and can stand with the filling exposed at the top.

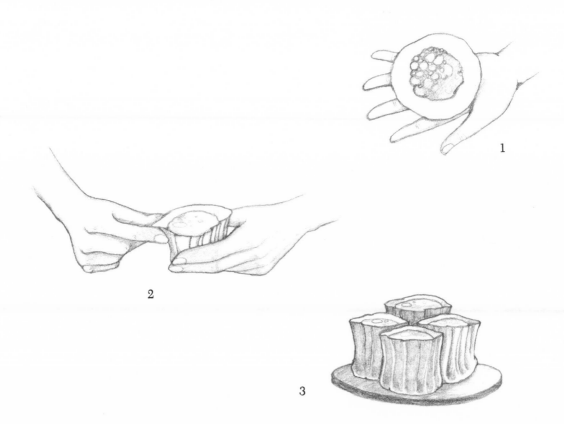

TO COOK:

5. Brush some oil on the bamboo steamer (if you do not have one, place the *shao mai* on a greased plate and put the plate on a steaming tray in the wok). Place the *shao mai* in the steamer, cover and steam over medium-high heat for 15 to 20 minutes and serve directly from the steamer.

NOTE: The *shao mai* can be made in advance and frozen for several weeks. They can also be kept, covered, in the refrigerator for 2 to 3 days.

Fried Dumplings (Guo Tie) 鍋貼

These fried dumplings are not really deep-fried. They are browned on the bottom and then steam-cooked with chicken broth. The result is delicious dumplings crispy on the bottom and fluffy soft on the top. When served with Hot and Sour Soup, they are a meal in themselves. In China they are a favorite food for lunch or for a mid-afternoon snack. The Chinese name for this kind of dumpling is "Guo Tie," which literally means "pot stickers."

INGREDIENTS:

4 cups sifted all-purpose flour
1 cup boiling water   } dough
⅔ cup cold water
½ lb (250 g) Chinese cabbage
2 tsp salt
3 to 5 dried Chinese mushrooms
¼ lb (125 g) uncooked shrimps, shelled
1 lb (500 g) ground pork
1 tsp ginger root, finely chopped   } filling
2 Tbs dark soy sauce
1½ tsp salt
2 Tbs sesame oil
2 Tbs chicken broth
1 Tbs Chinese rice wine
1 cup chicken broth
3 Tbs peanut or vegetable oil
¼ cup soy sauce   } dip
2 Tbs Chin Kiang vinegar

PROCEDURES:

1. Add boiling water to flour, mix with chopsticks; then add cold water gradually, and knead it very well until a smooth and soft dough results. Let stand for at least 15 minutes covered with a wet towel.

2. Wash the Chinese cabbage, drain, and chop very fine. Place the chopped cabbage in a bowl and sprinkle 2 tsp salt on it. Let stand for a few minutes; then squeeze out as much water as possible.

3. Soak the mushrooms in hot water until soft. Discard the stems and chop the mushrooms. Cut the shrimp into ¼-inch (6-mm) pieces.

4. In a large bowl, combine the ground pork, chopped cabbage, shrimp, mushrooms, ginger, soy sauce, salt, sesame oil, chicken broth, and wine. Mix thoroughly.

5. Remove the dough to a floured surface; knead again until smooth (2 to 3 minutes). Divide the dough into two parts, and with your hands, firmly shape each piece into a sausagelike cylinder about 12 inches (30 cm) long and 1 inch (2.5 cm) in diameter. Cut the roll of dough crosswise into ½-inch (1.5-cm) slices. Lay the slices on a lightly floured surface. Flatten each slice with the palm of your hand

and roll with a rolling pin into a disk about 3 inches (7.5 cm) in diameter and about ⅛ inch (3 mm) thick.

6. Place about 2 tsp of filling in the center of each wrapper; then fold over to make a half circle and pinch and pleat the edges together. Transfer the finished dumplings to a floured tray and keep it covered with a dry towel while you do the rest.

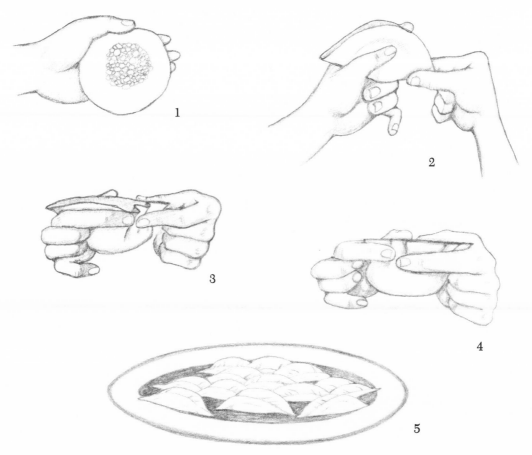

7. Set a 12-inch (30-cm) skillet over high heat for a few seconds. Pour in 2 Tbs oil and swirl it about in the pan. Place the dumplings, sides just touching, pleated side up, in the pan. Fry over medium heat for about 2 minutes or until the bottoms brown lightly. Add ½ cup chicken broth, cover the pan and cook over moderate heat for about 10 minutes or until the liquid has been absorbed.

8. Add 1 Tbs oil to side of pan and gently swirl it about in the skillet. Let the dumplings fry uncovered for 2 minutes longer. Place a round serving plate over the frying pan and invert the pan quickly. Serve the fried dumplings as soon as they are finished. If desired, combine the soy sauce and vinegar in a small bowl to be used as a dip or sauce for the dumplings.

NOTE: The dumplings (uncooked) can be made in advance and kept in the refrigerator for several hours. They can also be kept in the freezer for several weeks.

Steamed Dumplings 蒸餃

This is a famous Northern-style dumpling dish. Hot water and a little oil are used to make the soft, delicate dough. The unflavored gelatin makes the filling very juicy. Excellent for hors d'oeuvres, a hot lunch, or even a main course when served with a hearty soup.

INGREDIENTS:

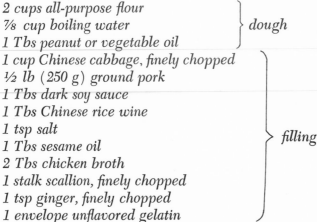

2 cups all-purpose flour
⅞ cup boiling water   } dough
1 Tbs peanut or vegetable oil

1 cup Chinese cabbage, finely chopped
½ lb (250 g) ground pork
1 Tbs dark soy sauce
1 Tbs Chinese rice wine
1 tsp salt
1 Tbs sesame oil   } filling
2 Tbs chicken broth
1 stalk scallion, finely chopped
1 tsp ginger, finely chopped
1 envelope unflavored gelatin

PROCEDURES:

1. Place the flour in a large bowl and gradually pour in the boiling water while stirring with chopsticks. Add 1 Tbs oil and stir until all the flour is damp and mealy. Let the dough cool, then knead until it is soft and smooth (add flour if it is too sticky). Cover the dough with a damp cloth and let it sit for 15 minutes.

2. Sprinkle ½ tsp salt on the chopped cabbage. Mix and set aside for 10 minutes. Then squeeze out the excess water.

3. Combine the ground pork with soy sauce, wine, salt, sesame oil, chicken broth, scallion, ginger, and unflavored gelatin. Mix well; then add the cabbage and mix some more.

4. Knead the dough again and divide into two parts. Keep one half covered and shape the other half into a sausagelike cylinder about 1 inch (2½ cm) in diameter. Cut into 15 pieces. Dust both sides of each piece with flour and press down with the palm of your hand. Use a rolling pin to roll each piece into a disk about 2½ inches (6 cm) in diameter and ⅛ inch (3 mm) thick.

5. Put about 1 Tbs filling in the center of each wrapper. Fold and pleat into half-moon-shaped dumplings.

TO COOK:

6. Line a bamboo steamer with slightly damp cheesecloth. Arrange the dumplings on the cloth; cover and steam over medium-high heat for 15 minutes. Serve in the steamer.

NOTE: The pleated dumplings can be placed on the steamer and kept refrigerated for several hours until ready to steam.

Stuffed Eggplant 茄子餅

See page 109 for this recipe.

Minced Shrimp in Lavor Rolls 紫菜蝦捲

This is a beautiful dish and excellent for hors d'oeuvres. The lavor is a purple sea-weed, as thin as transparent rice paper. Rich in iodine and sea flavor, it is often used for quick soup. It is also a favorite ingredient in Korean and Japanese cooking.

INGREDIENTS:
½ lb (250 g) raw shrimps, shelled and deveined
3 oz (90 g) pork fat, ground
1 stalk scallion, finely chopped ⎫
1 Tbs ginger root juice ⎪
½ Tbs Chinese rice wine ⎪
½ tsp salt ⎬ to marinate shrimps
½ egg white ⎪
1 tsp tapioca starch ⎭
3 sheets seaweed
½ lb (250 g) bok choy
½ tsp salt
¼ tsp sugar
½ Tbs Chinese rice wine
2 cups peanut oil or vegetable oil

PROCEDURES:
1. Crush the shrimps with one side of a cleaver. Add the ground pork fat and chop them fine. Marinate them in a bowl with scallion, ginger juice, wine, salt, egg white, and tapioca starch for about 30 minutes.

2. Cut each sheet of seaweed into 6 pieces. Place about ½ Tbs of shrimp mixture near the edge of the seaweed and roll into a tight roll, about the size of an index finger. Squeeze a little so that the shrimp mixture comes out a little on both sides. Use a little shrimp mixture to seal the outer edge to the roll. Set aside.

TO COOK:
3. Wash and then cut the bok choy into 1-inch (2.5-cm) pieces. Stir-fry in 2 Tbs oil in wok. Sprinkle in salt, sugar, and wine; stir and mix for about 2 minutes. Dish out on a serving platter.

4. Heat oil in the wok. Deep-fry the lavor rolls over medium heat for about 2 minutes until they are done. Remove and arrange around the bok choy on the platter.

NOTE: Watercress can be used instead of bok choy as the green in the center of the plate.

Paper-Wrapped Chicken 紙包鷄

See page 54 for this recipe.

Princess Chicken 龍芽鳳翼

See page 154 for this recipe.

Steamed Shrimp Dumplings (Har Gow) 蝦餃

Har gow is truly a Cantonese specialty. The dough is translucent and delicate, and the filling is tasty and crunchy with the chopped shrimp and fresh water chestnuts. It is one of the most popular *dim sum* served in the tea houses in China.

INGREDIENTS:

1 lb (500 g) raw shrimps, shelled and deveined, finely chopped
2 Tbs ground pork fat or fatty bacon, chopped
1 Tbs scallion (white part only), finely chopped
2 Tbs fresh water chestnuts, finely chopped
1 egg white
1 tsp tapioca starch
a little white pepper } *filling*
1 tsp salt
1 Tbs light soy sauce
1 Tbs Chinese rice wine
1 Tbs peanut oil or vegetable oil
1½ cups sifted wheat starch
½ cup sifted tapioca flour
1½ cups hot water } *to make the dough*
2 Tbs peanut or vegetable oil

PROCEDURES:

1. Combine the ingredients for the filling in a large bowl. Stir in one direction, mixing thoroughly. Refrigerate at least 1 hour.

2. Sift together the sifted wheat starch and tapioca flour into a large mixing bowl. Gradually add hot water, stirring constantly, then add peanut oil and let dough cool a little. Knead the dough until soft and smooth. Divide the dough in half. Keep one half covered in a bowl and place the other half on a lightly oiled surface. Knead, then roll into a sausagelike shape about 1 inch (2.5 cm) in diameter. Cut

crosswise into pieces ½ inch (1.5 cm) wide. Cover with a dry cloth to prevent the dough from drying out.

3. Brush some oil on one side of a cleaver, then flatten each small piece of dough between the blade and a flat surface by pressing evenly on the cleaver with the palm of your hand until the dough is very thin and about 2½ inches (6 cm) in diameter. (A small oiled rolling pin may be used to roll out the dough instead of a cleaver.)

4. Place 1 heaping teaspoon of shrimp filling in the center. Fold the edges together, pleating on one side.

TO COOK:

5. Place the *har gow* on the lightly greased bamboo steamer. First boil the water, then cover and steam for 5 minutes. Serve hot.

NOTE: Hot water should be added very gradually to the dough, with constant stirring and mixing. If the water is too hot, the dough will be too elastic; if the water is too cool, the dough will crack.

Steamed Roast Pork Buns 叉燒飽

Roast pork buns, known as *cha sio pao* to many Americans and Chinese alike, can be served as breakfast, lunch, snacks, or appetizers. They are a favorite mid-afternoon snack for Chinese children who return home from school hungry. Doughy on the outside, the filling is mellow with the tasty diced roast pork.

INGREDIENTS:

3½ cups all-purpose flour
½ package active dry yeast
    (about 1 tsp)
¼ cup lukewarm water   } dough
1 cup milk
2 Tbs sugar
½ tsp baking powder
½ lb (250 g) precooked Chinese
    roast pork (with some fat)
½ cup water
1½ Tbs flour
½ Tbs tapioca starch   } filling
1½ Tbs sugar
2 Tbs dark soy sauce
½ Tbs oyster sauce
½ Tbs sesame oil

PROCEDURES:

1. Place the flour in a large mixing bowl. In a separate bowl, combine the yeast with ¼ cup lukewarm water. Heat the milk to warm, add the sugar, and dissolve. Combine the yeast mixture with the milk, then slowly stir it into the flour to form a soft, firm dough. Knead until smooth and leave it in the bowl, covered with a damp cloth and let it rise in a warm place for 1½ to 2 hours or until doubled in bulk.

2. Cut the roast pork into thin slices, then cut each slice into pieces ¼ inch (6 mm) square. In a saucepan combine the water, flour, and tapioca starch. Stir to dissolve. Add the sugar, soy sauce, oyster sauce, and sesame oil. Heat and stir until mixture thickens. Add the pieces of roast pork and blend well. Let the filling cool.

3. Punch down the risen dough and turn it onto a lightly floured surface. Add the baking powder and knead for about 10 minutes or until the dough is smooth; sprinkle flour onto the dough from time to time while kneading. Roll the dough into a sausage-shape roll. Cut into 20 pieces each about 1½ inches (4 cm) in diameter. With the palm of the hand, flatten each into a circle, then roll each with a small rolling pin into a 3-inch (7.5-cm) disk. The center of each disk should be thicker than the edge.

4. Put about 1 heaping Tbs of filling in the center of each disk. Flute the edges of the disk and gather them together to form a pouch. Set each finished bun on

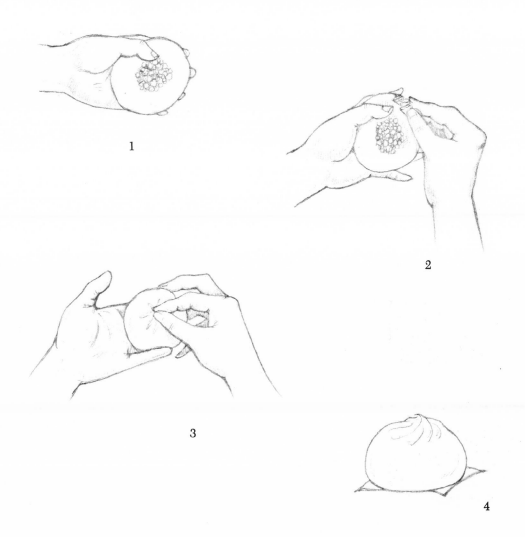

1

2

3

4

a square of waxed paper. Cover them as they are made and let rise for about 30 minutes.

TO COOK:

5. Bring the water in the steamer to a boil. Steam the buns over boiling water for about 15 minutes.

NOTE: The steamed roast pork buns can be kept in the freezer for a month. Reheat by steaming for 15 to 20 minutes.

PART VI

Chinese Desserts

The Chinese usually do not eat heavy pastries after a meal. Instead they often conclude a meal with either fresh fruit or a platter of canned lychees, longans, loquats, arbutus, or kumquats, served alone or mixed together. As a matter of fact, an assortment of these typical Chinese canned fruits goes well not only with Chinese meals but also with any cuisine in the world.

In a Chinese banquet, warm or cold sweets like Eight Precious Rice Pudding and Almond Float are usually served between courses to clear the palate and whet the appetite for the courses to follow. Chinese cakes are often small and light and are usually steamed rather than baked. They are used for snacks and between-meal entertaining rather than dessert. The recipes included here are relatively small in number, but they are excellent for both desserts and snacks.

Longan and Loquats Delight　龍眼批杷凍

INGREDIENTS:
one 15-oz (about 500-g) can loquats
one 15-oz (about 500-g) can longan
¼ cup sugar
1½ packages unflavored gelatin
½ cup cold water

PROCEDURES:
1. Remove the fruit from both cans and save the juice. Cut the loquats in half and mix them with the longan. Divide the fruit among 8 small custard cups.

2. Heat the juice from both cans and dissolve ¼ cup sugar in it. Dissolve the gelatin in ½ cup cold water and add it to the hot syrup; mix well. Fill each cup with this syrup and chill in the refrigerator until set (several hours).

3. To unmold before serving, place each cup in a flat pan filled with 1 inch (2.5 cm) of very hot water for a few seconds. Then immediately turn onto a dessert plate to unmold.

NOTE: This dish should be made one day ahead.

Almond Float 杏仁豆腐

INGREDIENTS:
1 envelope unflavored gelatin
⅓ cup cold water
¾ cup boiling water
⅓ cup sugar
1 cup homogenized milk
1 tsp almond extract
⅓ cup sugar
2 cups water } *to make additional syrup*
½ tsp almond extract
one 15-oz (about 500-g) can loquats
one 15-oz (about 500-g) can longans or lychees
one 15-oz (about 500-g) can arbutus

PROCEDURES:

1. Soften gelatin in ⅓ cup cold water. Add ¾ cup boiling water and ⅓ cup sugar. Stir until thoroughly dissolved. Pour in milk and almond extract. Mix well. Pour in cake pan and chill until set.

2. Mix ⅓ cup sugar with 2 cups of cold water and ½ tsp almond extract and chill to make additional syrup.

3. Cut the loquats in half. Pour the loquats and longans with the canning syrup into a big punch bowl. Drain the syrup from the can of arbutus (which would discolor the dish), and then add the arbutus to the big bowl.

4. Cut the almond float into ½-inch (1.5-cm) cubes or diamond-shaped pieces and mix them with the fruits in the bowl. Pour the additional syrup onto the mixture so that it can float. Serve in small individual rice bowls.

NOTE: The almond float should be made at least 5 or 6 hours and preferably one day ahead to allow sufficient time for it to set. Keep the finished dish in the refrigerator until ready to serve. This is a light and refreshing dessert, excellent even after a heavy meal.

Sweet-Filled Wontons (Golden Surprise) 芝麻棗泥雲吞

INGREDIENTS:

8-oz (250-g) package pitted red dates
2 Tbs sesame seeds
½ cup dark corn syrup
1 package wonton wrappers
2 cups peanut oil or vegetable oil
confectioner's sugar

PROCEDURES:

1. Cook the red dates in ½ cup water for about 20 minutes. Grind dates and sesame seeds. Moisten with syrup.

2. Place about ½ tsp date and sesame seed mixture in the center of each wonton and fold and wrap into the shape of a nurse's cap. (For illustration on folding, see the recipe for Wonton in Soup, page 28.)

TO COOK:

3. Deep-fry the wontons in oil at medium-high heat until golden brown. Remove to paper towels and cool slightly. Sprinkle with confectioner's sugar. Serve cool.

NOTE: This sweet-filled wonton can be kept for several weeks in a tightly covered can.

Banana Stuffed with Sweet Red Bean Paste 豆沙香蕉

INGREDIENTS:
6 bananas (just ripe)
8 Tbs sweet red bean paste
1 cup all-purpose flour
2 Tbs tapioca starch
1 cup water
2 tsp baking powder
2 cups peanut or vegetable oil
¼ cup sugar

PROCEDURES:

1. Peel bananas. Split lengthwise and make a small groove in both halves. Stuff about 1 Tbs red bean paste between each 2 banana halves. Join halves, then cut each banana into 1½-inch (4-cm) sections. Set aside.

2. Mix the flour and tapioca starch in a bowl. Add water gradually and mix into a smooth batter. Mix in the baking powder. (The consistency of the batter should be rather thick.)

TO COOK:

3. Heat the wok, add oil, and heat to 350° F (177° C). Dip the banana sandwiches in the batter. Fry 7 to 8 pieces at a time until golden brown, about 6 to 8 minutes. Drain, sprinkle sugar on top, and serve.

NOTE: The fried bananas can be reheated in a preheated 400° F (204° C) oven for 10 minutes.

Red Dates and Sesame Seed Ping 紅棗芝麻餅

INGREDIENTS:
8-oz (250-g) package pitted red dates
4 Tbs sesame seeds
½ cup dark corn syrup
1 roll frozen biscuit dough
2 egg whites

PROCEDURES:

1. Cook the red dates in ½ cup water for about 20 minutes. Grind dates with 2 Tbs sesame seeds and moisten with the syrup. This is the filling.

2. Divide roll of frozen dough into 10 pieces and cut each piece in half. Roll dough out to round shape about 1½ inch (4 cm) in diameter.

3. Place about 1 tsp of filling in the center of each round dough. Pinch edges together and flatten slightly.

4. Dip one surface in the egg white and then in the remaining 2 Tbs of sesame seeds.

TO COOK:

5. Preheat oven to 350° F (177° C).

6. With the sesame seed side up, arrange the 20 pings on a cookie sheet. Bake for 10 to 12 minutes. Serve hot or cold.

NOTE: "Ping" means "cake." These small delicate cakes with red dates and sesame seeds are excellent snacks.

Eight Precious Rice Pudding 八寶飯

INGREDIENTS:
10 red dates
10 mixed dried fruits
1 cup glutinous rice (sweet rice)
1 cup cold water
2 tsp sugar
2 Tbs lard or peanut oil
⅔ cup canned sweet red bean paste
1 cup water ⎫
½ cup sugar ⎪
2 tsp almond extract ⎬ *sauce*
2 tsp tapioca starch dissolved in 2 tsp water ⎭

PROCEDURES:

1. Cook the red dates in ½ cup water over low heat for 30 minutes. When soft, cut the dates in halves and set aside.

2. Wash the glutinous rice and drain. Place the rice in a saucepan, add 1 cup of water and bring to a boil. Cover and simmer for about 15 minutes. Mix the warm rice with sugar and oil.

3. Spread a large piece of clear plastic wrap on the bottom of a shallow bowl (about 3 cups capacity). Take ⅔ of the cooked rice and line the bottom and the sides of the bowl on top of the plastic wrap. Spread the red bean paste in a layer over the rice. Cover the red bean paste with the remaining rice. To decorate, invert the rice pudding onto a plate and make a design with the dates and mixed fruit. Carefully cover the pudding with the same plastic wrap and then the bowl, and flip back into the bowl.

TO COOK:

4. Steam the rice pudding over a moderate heat for at least 1 hour. Invert the pudding onto a plate.

5. Make the sauce by combining the water, sugar, and almond extract in a small saucepan. Bring to a boil. Stir in the tapioca starch and water mixture to thicken. Pour the sauce over the pudding and serve hot.

NOTE: This classic dessert can be made in advance, steamed until done, and left in the shallow bowl. Reheat by steaming again for about ½ hour. Flip the pudding onto a plate, pour the glazed sauce on top and serve hot. Any number of fruits may be added, such as sugared lotus seeds, gingko nuts, dried or canned lychees, canned loquats, and raisins.

APPENDICES

Appendix 1

SAMPLE SUGGESTED MENUS

A distinctive feature of Chinese meals is that there is no one "main course." Instead, a great variety of food is served. Normally, an average meal for 4 to 6 people consists of four dishes—one meat or poultry dish, one fish or other seafood dish, and two vegetable dishes—as well as soup and rice or buns. Actually it is much more nutritious and more fun to eat such a great variety of food in one meal. But there are some important rules to bear in mind when planning Chinese meals:

1. Do not plan more than two last-minute, stir-fried dishes in one meal. Different cooking methods and techniques should be employed for cooking convenience. For example, choose some dishes that can be cooked ahead of time and then reheated, such as red-cooked or stewed dishes. There are also many dishes that can be precooked in parts and then cooked together at the last minute. One may also use cold mixing or cold dishes for a delightful change. Oven-ready or steamed dishes are also easy to serve. In other words, the planning and preparation of a meal should be so organized as to avoid last-minute chaos.

2. It is also important to harmonize and balance flavor, color, and texture. For instance, a hot and spicy dish should be accompanied by a mild, subtle one. If one dish is dry, such as a deep-fried or dry-cooked dish, there should be one dish that has some sauce to balance it. Some foods are cooked soft, whereas other dishes should remain firm and crisp.

3. Plan a balanced diet through a great variety of food. For example, mix the meat dish from the northern region with the seafood of the eastern area and the stir-fried vegetables of Canton. Another point to remember is that although fresh ingredients are desirable, Chinese preserved foods have their place, too. Preserved foods, with their distinctive tastes and textures, are very important in Chinese cooking.

4. A simplified family meal may consist of two dishes—one meat, poultry, or fish and one vegetable. But it is important to choose recipes that use a greater variety of ingredients. For example, beef can be stir-fried with snow peas, water chestnuts, and baby corn, and bean curd can be cooked with meat.

The following are sample menus for 4 to 6 people when you entertain; they can also be used for large families of 6 to 8 people. Rice or steamed buns and tea should be served with the dishes. These menus are quite flexible. If you have fewer than 6 people, you can eliminate one or two dishes from the list; if you have more than 6 people, one or two more dishes can be added, or the quantity of some dishes can be doubled.

I   Empress Chicken
Spicy Shredded Beef with Cellophane Noodles
Steamed Fish with Fermented Black Beans
Agar-Agar Salad with Ham
Fish Balls and Bean Thread Soup
Almond Float

II   Lion's Head
Dry-Cooked String Beans
Shrimp with Cashew Nuts
Chicken Slices with Straw Mushrooms and Snow Peas
Winter Melon with Ham Soup
Longan and Loquats Delight

III   Sweet and Sour Spareribs
Sautéed Bean Curd, Family Style
Braised Soy Sauce Chicken
Bok Choy with Bamboo Shoots and Mushrooms
Peking Hot and Sour Soup
Mixed Fruit with Lychee, Loquats, and Arbutus

IV   Steamed Pearl Balls
Meat Platter in Three Colors
Sweet and Sour Cabbage, Szechuan Style
Bean Curd with Straw Mushrooms
Fish Balls and Bean Thread Soup
Bananas Stuffed with Red Bean Paste

V   Spiced Pork
Fish-Flavored Chicken
Snow Peas with Bamboo Shoots and Mushrooms
Stir-Fried Rice Noodles with Shrimp and Vegetables
Shark's Fin Soup
Eight Precious Rice Pudding

The following are sample suggested menus for 2 to 4 people:

I   Roast Pork Lomein
Bok Choy with Bamboo Shoots and Mushrooms
Wontons in Soup

II   Beef in Oyster Sauce with Snow Peas and Water Chestnuts
Chinese Cabbage in Cream Sauce
Peking Hot and Sour Soup

III   Steamed Fish, Hunan Style
      Mu Shu Pork with Pancakes
      Agar-Agar Salad with Ham

IV   Chinese Fried Noodles, Both Sides Brown
      Chicken with Nuts in Hoisin Sauce
      Ma Po Bean Curd

V   Fried Chicken Slices with Lemon Sauce
      Sweet and Sour Cabbage, Szechuan Style
      Yangchow Fried Rice

Appendix 2

BASIC CUTTING TECHNIQUES

In Chinese cooking, most of the ingredients are first cut into bite-size pieces before cooking. Therefore, to learn how to cut properly and efficiently is extremely important. One of the indispensable utensils the cook will need is a cleaver. The cleaver can be used to slice, shred, dice, mince, chop, tenderize, and flatten food, and even grind with the wooden handle. Without the cleaver, a cook would need a great variety of knives to do the different jobs required in Chinese cooking.

The cleaver provides both weight, important for chopping and mincing, and dexterity, essential to thin slicing and fine shredding. Furthermore, all parts of the cleaver are useful. The sharp edge of the cleaver is used to slice, shred, dice, mince, roll-cut, and chop. The blunt edge of the cleaver is used to tenderize meat by pounding the meat in a crisscross pattern. The flat side of the cleaver can be used to slap the meat and to crush items like ginger and garlic. The wooden handle also has its own use—to grind or pound ingredients into powder form. In addition, after cutting one can use the flat side of the cleaver as a spatula to lift the cut pieces into a dish. Chinese cleavers come in different weights and sizes, but the best choice is the number 3 or 4 carbon steel cleaver, which can be used to cut meat as well as vegetables.

To cut with the cleaver, place the food on a chopping board. Hold the cleaver firmly with your right hand, with the thumb and forefinger falling on either side of the blade. With the left hand, hold and press in place the items to be cut, but make sure that the first joints of the fingers stick out and the fingertips are hidden. This way you will not have any accidents because your fingertips are curved inward. Remember also the cutting motion is not just an up-and-down motion. It is a forward and downward motion, with the strength coming from the shoulder.

Here are some basic ways of cutting:

SLICING:
There are two kinds: straight slicing and slant slicing. Straight slicing is done with the cleaver perpendicular to the items to be sliced. The slices should generally be very thin. Slant slicing is done with the cleaver at a 45-degree angle to the food. This method of slicing is used whenever you want to cut thin, wide slices from flat or small items.

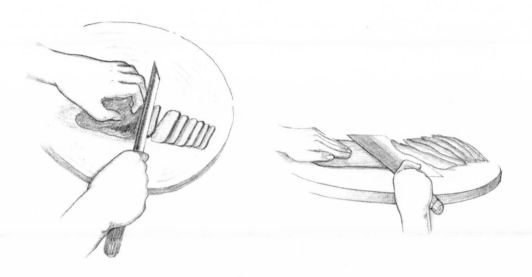

SHREDDING:
First cut the food into thin slices and then cut these slices into uniform strips about 2 inches (5 cm) long. Several slices may be piled on top of one another before shredding.

DICING:

First cut the food lengthwise into strips about ¼ inch (6 mm) to ½ inch (1.5 cm) wide, then cut these strips into small cubes or dice.

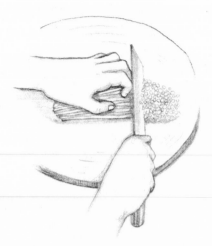

MINCING:

First slice, then shred, and then cut the shreds into very fine pieces.

ROLL-CUTTING:

Roll-cutting is done to expose a greater number of food surfaces, allowing food to cook faster and flavor to be absorbed more easily. To roll-cut a carrot, first make a slant slice. Then roll the carrot a quarter turn so that the cut surface faces upward. Slice diagonally through the cut surface. Then roll the carrot another quarter turn and repeat the process until all the carrot is cut into oblique pieces.

Appendix 3

BASIC COOKING METHODS

Many Americans hesitate to try Chinese cooking because they think all Chinese food is stir-fried at the last minute. The question is often raised, "How can I cook two or three dishes at the same time?"

Although stir-frying is the most common method used in Chinese cooking, it is definitely not the *only* method. Many well-known dishes are cooked by the following methods as well.

STEAMING:

Steaming by wet heat is a frequently used method. Steamers, as are ovens in the Western world, are important cooking utensils. In steaming, the food is placed on a dish or directly on the steamer which is suspended over boiling water and the whole thing is covered. The intense steam from the boiling water circulates and cooks the food. Steaming often intensifies the taste of seasoned food, and it is also a very healthy way of cooking since oil is not usually used. Steamed Fish with Fermented Black Beans, Steamed Pearl Balls, Steamed Spareribs with Spicy Rice Powder, and all kinds of steamed dumplings are perfect examples.

RED-COOKING:

Red-cooking, or Chinese stewing, is frequently used in Eastern-style cooking. The food is simmered slowly in dark soy sauce, which gives it a deep reddish color. Star anise, five-spice powder, ginger, and scallion are often used to give a dish its distinctive aroma, and rice wine and rock sugar are used for the mellow taste and the glazed sauce. Red-Cooked Duck, Braised Soy Sauce Chicken, and Sweet and Sour Spareribs exemplify this type of cooking. An advantage of the red-cooked method is that the dish can be cooked in advance and reheated before serving. The flavor often intensifies in reheating.

PARBOILING:

Parboiling is often used to prepare vegetables before they are stir-fried. To parboil any vegetable, first bring the water in a saucepan to a boil. Add the vegetable to the boiling water; without covering the saucepan, bring to a boil again. Then immediately rinse the vegetable under cold water until cool. After being parboiled, most vegetables take only a few seconds to stir-fry; the bright green color is set; and the raw taste is gone.

CLEAR-SIMMERING:

Clear-simmering means cooking the ingredients in broth over low heat until the ingredients are tender and the soup flavorful. Salt and rice wine are usually added at the end, and the natural flavor of food is captured. Winter Melon with Ham Soup and Odd-Flavor Chicken are done by the clear-simmering method.

DEEP-FRYING:

Deep-frying is a process shared by most cuisines. The food is cooked in deep hot oil until it is golden brown and thoroughly cooked. But the difference in Chinese deep-frying is that it is not just used as an end in itself to cook the food and serve. Often it is used as a preparatory step before the ingredients are stir-fried and seasoned to serve. For example, in Sautéed Bean Curd, Family Style and Dry-Cooked String Beans, the bean curd or string beans are first deep-fried before they are stir-fried.

SHALLOW-FRYING:

Shallow-frying is similar to French sautéing. Food is seared slowly in hot oil over medium heat for several minutes and then turned over to brown the other side. This method is often used for food that has already been partially cooked, as in the case of Chinese Fried Noodle, Both Sides Brown.

STIR-FRYING:

Last but not least, stir-frying is the most frequently used method in Chinese cooking. It means that small pieces of food are tossed and turned continuously over high heat in a small amount of oil and for a short period of time. Since most ingredients are cut into bite-size pieces before stir-frying, the cooking time is short, fuel is saved, and nutritious vitamins and minerals are preserved. Successful stir-frying takes careful preparation of ingredients in advance and vigilance during cooking. You must be ready to adjust the heat and timing instantly. Though it may seem a little nerve-racking in the beginning, with practice, it will become a most delightful cooking method.

Appendix 4

CHINESE COOKING UTENSILS

Proper cooking utensils not only make cooking easier, they also give the cook more confidence and more fun. The following are some of the basic utensils needed for Chinese cooking.

No Chinese cook would consider his kitchen equipment complete without woks, cleavers, and chopsticks. A wok is the most ingenious and versatile cooking utensil. Since it is roomy and round-bottomed, food can be tossed and stirred easily in it. It can also be used to prepare red-cooked dishes and as a base in steaming. In the morning it is an excellent utensil in which to fry or scramble eggs. American frozen or fresh vegetables can be stir-fried in the wok instead of being boiled to death.

Cooking teachers usually do not recommend getting stainless steel, aluminum, or electric woks. The best wok to get is the heavy-duty, carbon-steel wok, and the most practical size is the 14-inch diameter. A wok with a long wooden handle is quite handy since you can hold onto the handle while stir-frying without burning your hand. Flat-bottomed woks are generally recommended for electric stoves.

When you acquire a new wok, it is important to season it before using it, to prevent food from sticking and the metal from rusting. First wash off the mechanical oil both inside and out with hot water and detergent. (Manufacturers often coat the woks with cheap mechanical oil to protect them.) To season the wok, first wipe it dry, then coat the entire interior surface of the wok with a little vegetable oil; heat the oil on medium heat for 1 minute while tilting and rotating the wok; wipe off the oil with a paper towel. Repeat this process (coat with oil, heat over medium heat, and wipe with paper towel). Now the wok is ready to be used. A wok that is well-seasoned by constant use will never rust. But do coat the wok with a little oil before storage if you do not use it often. After the wok has been treated, do not use detergent to wash it. Just scrub the wok with a hard brush under hot running water. The best way to dry the wok is to place it on the stove over medium heat for several minutes until it is completely dry.

A ring is used to keep the round-bottomed wok steady over the flat-surfaced stove.

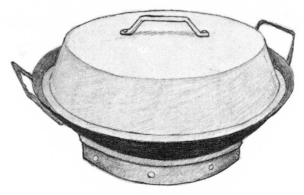

A cleaver is indispensable in Chinese cooking. Please see Appendix 2 Basic Cutting Techniques (page 188) for the uses of a cleaver and methods of cutting.

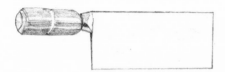

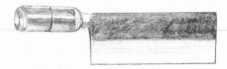

A steamer set is equally important in Chinese cooking since steaming is one of the major cooking methods. Two kinds of steamers are available: the bamboo and the aluminum steamer set. A bamboo steamer set ventilates well in steaming and, since it is a beautiful utensil, most steamed food (dumplings, pearl balls, and spare-ribs, for example) can be served directly from the steamer. The aluminum steamer set includes a bottom pot to hold water, and hence it does not need to be set over a wok, as does the bamboo set. But the food needs to be transferred onto a serving platter before serving.

Before use, a new bamboo steamer should be placed over a wok of boiling water for one hour in order to remove the bamboo smell. A pot of boiling water should be kept ready to add to the wok when necessary.

Chinese spatulas, ladles, chopsticks, wired sieves, and a good chopping board are also important in order to make the cooking easier and enjoyable.

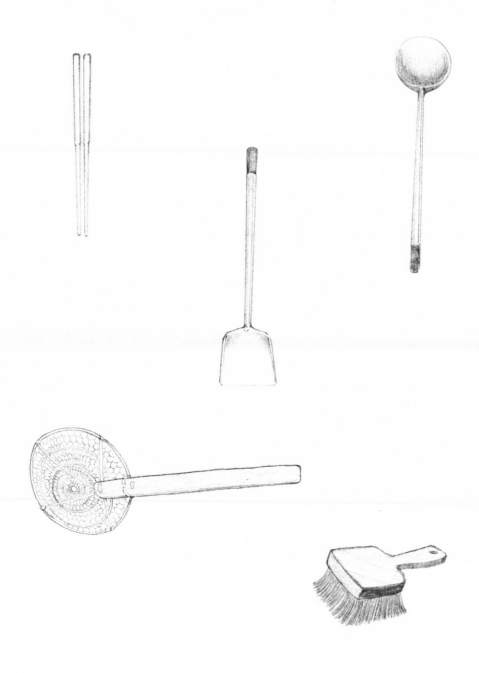

Appendix 5

HOW TO COOK PERFECT RICE

Rice is extremely important in China not only because it symbolizes livelihood but also because it is the foundation of the Chinese diet. The majority of Chinese eat rice three times a day, and there are people, especially Southerners, who would feel that they have not eaten or would still feel hungry if they did not have a bowl of white rice with their meal.

Since rice is an integral part of daily meals, there are many dishes created mainly to "send down the rice." There are also many dishes whose flavors cannot be fully appreciated unless contrasted with the natural taste of rice. Much of the familiar slang used in China also shows the importance of rice. For example, the first greeting between friends is not "How are you?" but "Have you eaten rice?" When dinner is ready, the announcement is "Rice is ready!" Children are often advised and warned not to waste a single grain of rice otherwise they might starve in the next life.

Since rice is so important in Chinese lives, naturally it is important to learn how to cook perfect rice. The Chinese never use salt or butter in cooking rice. The right amount of water is important though in order to make a lovely, light, fluffy rice. Follow the measurements and methods below closely, and you will be able to get the desired result.

Long Grain Rice	Water
1 cup	1¾ cup
2 cups	3¼ cups
3 cups	4 cups
4 cups	5 cups

Short Grain Rice	Water
1 cup	1½ cups
2 cups	2½ cups
3 cups	3⅞ cups

Measure the rice into a large saucepan and rinse it once in cold water. Drain and add the proper amount of water to the rice. Bring to a boil, then turn to low heat, cover and simmer for 20 minutes. At end of 20 minutes, turn off the heat and let the rice "relax" and continue to cook in its own heat for 20 more minutes. Loosen before serving. Once cooked, the rice will stay hot in the saucepan for about 30 minutes. It may also be put into a serving dish, covered, and placed in a warm oven for 30 minutes without drying out. If the rice is cold, it can be reheated by placing it in a bowl and steaming.

The long grain rice is most often used in restaurants because it is firmer after cooking and the result is better when used in fried rice. The short grain rice is softer and stickier, and is excellent for making breakfast rice congees.

With the invention of the electric rice cooker, rice cooking becomes easier and simpler. The electric cooker is used by practically all Oriental families both in America and in the Orient and by many Americans. It is easy to use, reliable, cooks rice automatically, and keeps it warm for hours. Furthermore, it saves the use of a burner when one is entertaining. It is a most practical and wonderful appliance for a Chinese kitchen.

ABOUT THE AUTHOR

Mrs. Lucille Liang, of a distinguished Mainland Chinese family that went to Taiwan after the civil war, now operates a Chinese Cooking School and is owner of Liang's Oriental Gifts and Grocery Inc. in Pleasantville, N.Y. She has also taught Chinese cooking at the Scarsdale Adult Education School and at the YWCA in White Plains, and has been invited to give lectures and demonstrations about Chinese food all over Westchester County and Connecticut.

Born in Szechuan, Mrs. Liang grew up in Shanghai, Canton, Hong Kong, and Taiwan. She can speak five different dialects and has sampled authentic dishes from different regions of China. After having received her B.A. in English from National Taiwan University, she and her husband Grant Liang came to the United States for graduate study. Subsequently she received her M.A. in English from Brooklyn College as well as an Artist's Degree in voice and music from Westchester Conservatory of Music.

Mrs. Liang worked as an editor at Holt, Rinehart and Winston Inc. in New York and at Garrard Publishing Company in Scarsdale, N.Y. She has done freelance editing for many publishing companies, including Harper & Row, Publishers, McGraw-Hill, Pergamon Press, and Academic Press.

Moved by the enthusiasm of her American friends to learn Chinese cooking and encouraged by many who have tasted her cooking and tried her recipes, Mrs. Liang decided to open a Chinese Cooking School and a Chinese grocery store for the convenience of those who want to cook Chinese food. Those who have taken lessons from her now number well over a thousand, and both men and women flock to her famed cooking school from all over New York, Connecticut, and Westchester County.

Inspired and encouraged by all her students who have tested her recipes, Mrs. Liang decided to compile her authentic recipes to form a cookbook which offers not only tasty, nutritious, and enjoyable recipes but also cultural and historical background about the dishes. Furthermore, for the first time an American can easily find his or her favorite exotic dishes from Szechuan, Shanghai, Peking, or Canton by simply turning to the particular chapter on that region. The recipes are grouped by the four major schools of cooking in China. Mrs. Liang hopes that her cookbook will bring joy and good food to her students as well as to thousands of others who do not have the chance to come to her cooking school.

INDEX

chicken slices with straw mushrooms and snow peas, 64

chicken, stir-fried, diced, in bird's nest, 76-77

chicken with nuts in hoisin sauce, 63

chicken with walnuts, 143

duck, Peking, 80-81

duck, red-cooked, 44

dumplings, Peking, with pork and vegetables, 160-161

dumplings, steamed, 168

dumplings, steamed shrimp, 170-171

eggplant, stuffed, 109

eggplant, Szechuan, 101

fish, crispy spicy, 115-116

fish, fillet, with wine rice sauce, 75

fish, fried whole, in sweet and sour sauce, 78-79

fish, smoked, Soochow style, 51

fish, soy sauce, Shanghai style, 26

fish, squirrel, 56-57

fish, steamed, Hunan style, 91

fish, steamed, with fermented black beans, 128

fish wrapped in dried bean curd sheet rolls, 52-53

lion's head, 30-31

meat platter in three colors, 37-38

melon, stuffed winter, with ham, 49-50

mushrooms, Chinese, stuffed with pork and water chestnuts, 159

noodles, Chinese fried, both sides brown, 138-139

noodles, stir-fried rice, with shrimps and vegetables, 34

pork, *mu shu*, with pancakes, 67-68

pork (or beef), shredded, in hot sauce, 97-98

pork, shredded, in Peking sauce, 73

pork, shredded, with bean threads, 24

pork, spiced, 36

pork, twice-cooked, 106

prawns (or shrimps), dry-cooked, Szechuan style, 104

rice cakes, stir-fried, 41-42

rice, seafood sizzling, 107-108

rice, shrimp fried, Cantonese style, 123

rice, Yangchow fried, 39-40

scallops and Chinese radish balls, 47

shao mai, steamed, 164-165

shrimp balls, deep fried, 43

shrimp in lobster sauce, 136

shrimp, minced, in lavor rolls, 169

shrimps, dried, and bean threads soup, 66

shrimps, Szechuan style, 99

shrimp, stir-fried lovers', 134

shrimp toasts, 71

shrimp with cashew nuts, 131

soup, assorted delicacies, in winter melon, 150-151

soup, Peking hot and sour, 69-70

soup, shark's fin, 148-149

spareribs, steamed, with spicy rice powder, 100

spareribs, sweet and sour, 27

spareribs, with fermented black beans, 137

spring rolls, Shanghai, 162-163

squid, sweet and sour, 32-33

string beans, dry-cooked, 86

wonton in soup, 28-29

Roast Pork Lomein, 119

roll cutting, 190

rolls, lavor, *see* lavor rolls

salads
  agar-agar, with ham, 22
  cabbage, Chinese, with hot chili oil, 74
  noodle, cold, with sesame paste sauce, 35

sausages, Chinese
  chicken and rice, 120-121

Sautéed Bean Curd, Family Style, 87

Sautéed Mixed Vegetables, 48

SCALLIONS
  ants on the trees, 85
  bean curd, sautéed, family style, 87
  bean curd, *Ma Po*, 90
  bean curd, stuffed, Cantonese style, 144-145
  bean curd with straw mushrooms, 122
  beef and broccoli in oyster sauce, 130
  beef in oyster sauce with snow peas and water chestnuts, 124-125
  beef, orange flavor, 113-114
  beef, steamed, with spicy rice powder, 105
  chicken and Chinese sausage rice, 120-121
  chicken, bon bon, 102-103
  chicken, fish-flavored, 95-96
  chicken, odd-flavor, 110-112
  chicken, princess, 154-155
  chicken, shredded, with bean sprouts, 72
  chicken, stir-fried diced, in birds nest, 76-77
  curling, 81
  duck, Peking, 80-81
  duck, red-cooked, 44
  dumplings, Peking, pork and vegetables, 160-161
  dumplings, steamed, 168
  dumplings, steamed shrimp, 170-171
  eggplant, stuffed, 109
  eggplant, Szechuan style, 101
  fish balls and bean threads soup, 23
  fish, crispy spicy, 115-116
  fish, fried whole, in sweet and sour sauce, 78-79
  fish, smoked, Soochow style, 51
  fish, soy sauce, Shanghai style, 26
  fish, steamed, Hunan style, 91
  fish, steamed, with fermented black beans, 128
  fish wrapped in dried bean curd sheet rolls, 52-53
  lion's head, 30-31
  melon, winter, stuffed, with ham, 49-50
  noodles salad, cold, with sesame paste sauce, 35
  pearl balls, steamed, 92
  pork lomein, roast, 119
  pork, *mu shu*, with pancakes, 67-68
  pork, shredded, in Peking sauce, 73
  pork (or beef), shredded, in hot sauce, 97-98
  pork, shredded, with bean threads, 24
  prawns, dry-cooked, Szechuan style, 104
  rice noodles, stir-fried, with shrimps and vegetables, 34
  rice, shrimp fried, Cantonese style, 123
  rice, Yangchow fried, 39-40
  shao mai, steamed, 164-165
  shrimp in lobster sauce, 136
  shrimp, minced, in lavor rolls, 169
  shrimps, dried, and bean threads soup, 66
  shrimp, stir-fried lovers', 134
  shrimp, Szechuan style, 99
  shrimp with cashew nuts, 131
  soup, Peking hot and sour, 69-70
  soup, three kinds of shredded delicacy, 46
  spareribs, steamed, with spicy rice noodles, 100
  spareribs, sweet and sour, 27

yellow croaker, Chinese
    fish, crispy spicy, 115-116
    fish, fried whole, in sweet and sour sauce, 78-79
    fish, squirrel, 56-57

yellow pike
    fish, fillet, with wine rice sauce, 75
    fish, squirrel, 56-57